MUSIC
OBSERVED

MUSIC
OBSERVED

by

A. H. FOX-STRANGWAYS

THE SELECTION MADE BY STEUART WILSON

Essay Index Reprint Series

BOOKS FOR LIBRARIES PRESS, INC.
FREEPORT, NEW YORK

First Published 1936
Reprinted 1968

LIBRARY OF CONGRESS CATALOG CARD NUMBER:
68-16931

PREFACE

By STEUART WILSON

THE object of a preface is, as a rule, to introduce to the public the work of an unknown author, whose excellence shall be guaranteed by appearing under such wings of fame as may be spread by the "prefator". Here the position is neatly reversed, for Mr. Fox Strangways has been a musical journalist for twenty-five years, and has written a round thousand articles on music, whereas I, who so cheerfully "introduce" him, am a whole generation his junior, and caused my sole undergraduate enterprise in musical criticism to come to a sudden and unpremeditated close with an action for libel.

In the literary world of to-day authors and critics lie down and eat straw together quietly by virtue of their functions having become so mingled that A reviews B's novel with the certainty that in a short time B will be having his way with A "in another place". For the musical world we performers can seldom get the chance of criticizing our critics, and indeed we hardly know them except as a black-avised gang of Beckmessers who sit in the back row of concert-halls. But they are (as the Lancashire wife said of her husband) "not so bad when you get to know them", and my friendships have taught me amongst other things that some of our critics "know their stuff" better than we performers believe them to. Our respect for their judgment is also increased when we know that they have been in touch with any of the actualities of musical life as we performers know it. We may be wrong in this opinion, for perhaps aesthetic judgments can be formed without any inside knowledge of processes—but we like tu think that a critic knows from some experience of his own.

We know that men are "trained" for the musical profession, but that they "drift" into journalism, and Mr. Fox Strangways is no exception. After Balliol he went to the Hochschule at Berlin and returned to this country to teach not music as it fell out, but German at Dulwich and subsequently at Wellington. After ten years of ordinary schoolmastering, when Alan Gray left Wellington for Trinity College, Cambridge, the organ stool and the conductor's baton passed to A. H. F. S. Temporary dislocations of health caused him to leave Wellington and to seek health by two visits to India, the fruit of which was *The Music of Hindustan*, a work of exact observation and scholarship now safe in its niche in the libraries of the world, but "out of print". Upon his final return from India he joined the staff of *The Times* in 1911, thus beginning a new career at the age when many of us are looking for fields and pastures only to go to grass in. In 1920 he wanted yet more room to

spread himself and *Music and Letters* came into being
—the longest-lived private musical journal in this
country. In that same year I was first introduced to him,
a young man who was interested in the problem of
translating German songs, and our collaboration remains
the pleasantest form of work that ever comes my way.
In 1925 *The Observer* called him away from Printing
House Square, and long may he "observe music" from
that pinnacle.

For the rest, I would merely explain that I am responsible for the selection of the articles chosen, not from
all that the learned author has written, but from such as
have survived a certain incompleteness of business
habits and found themselves lodged, such as they are
and often undated, in large envelopes sorted according
to general categories, in which they are here reprinted.
It is meant to be a "browsing" book, to be read at ease
and at leisure—perhaps even in bed—but without
the necessity of leaping to the bookshelf or to the piano.

And with this Prologue let the curtain go up.

                                            STEUART WILSON

ACKNOWLEDGMENT

THE thanks of the Author and Editor are due to the proprietors of *The Observer*, the *London Mercury*, and *Music and Letters* for permission to reprint the articles (or parts of them) which originally appeared in those publications.

CONTENTS

BYPATHS

NEW WORKS

CRITICISM

TECHNIQUE

SUNDRIES

MUSIC OBSERVED

ON THE WRITING OF ARTICLES

THE writer of an article is often at a loss as to how to begin. If we, his readers, have watched ourselves at all, we know that we have as a rule glanced at his title and skipped his first page or two, on to where, about the bottom of page three, something caught our eye. We hunt that trail for a dozen lines and dip again somewhere else. If both were lucky draws, we put the thing down with—"I must read that some time or other" —and perhaps we do.

The trouble, then, is the beginning. We should *like* to begin . . . "I say, have you ever noticed that", or, "how . . ." but that would be a little *too* undress. It would be sincere, though; because most articles that are at all readable arise out of conversations, if not heated arguments, with friends. After one of those we feel ourselves "fit to write". Our brain simply seethes with clinching proofs and dazzling instances, and we hardly know which to choose. It must clearly be something arresting. Shall it be, Macaulay-like, a profound truism—"History, at least in its ideal state of perfection, is a compound of poetry and philosophy"? Or a pregnant story—"A pious Brahmin, it is written, made a vow that on a certain day he would . . ."? Or, in his desire to be all things to all men in the hope of winning some, shall the writer imitate the boy who, being warned by his father that he must get people's attention at once, began his short-story with—" 'Damn your eyes,' said the Duchess, as she passed the potatoes"—thus epitomizing his knowledge of human nature in one abrupt, alliterative antithesis of high and low life. Well, having written his proem by one of these means, or by some other, the best advice that can be given him is that he should subject it to severe compression. He probably will not take the advice; but there is still some hope that his editor will restore the balance with a pair of scissors.

At last he is off, with his sail spread to the breeze. The first thing he discovers is that he knows some parts of his subject better than others. It is not good, certainly, to write of what one does not know, and there are plenty of acceptable articles containing only those things which the writer does know. Still, it is better to fill the gaps, even if it means reading a stout volume or two to do it. There is no hurry, and we want this article to be as good as we can make it. But if we feast at other people's tables, we must leave time for digestion. The facts or arguments are nothing until assimilated.

His next experience, perhaps, is that he finds himself proving the wrong point. The best cure for that is to tear up the sheet at once and begin again. There is no patching or correcting such things, because even if he can find the word or phrase that actually started him on the wrong scent, which is not easy to do, the getting the rest of it to match the correction is only useless trouble: the passage will still look chequered.

The article is to be as good as we can make it, but it can never be final. When we look at a collection of old "Greats" essays, two things strike us. First, what a wonderful deal we knew in those days, and second, how much better use we could make of it now. From the fact that we have learnt a little about how to express things, we may argue that there is room to learn more; that the article we write at thirty may easily be bettered by one we shall write at forty. And herein lies the chief argument for writing articles at all. That great book that we mean to write one day "when we can find some time"—on quaternions, or edible fungi, or tonality— will, of course, be final. It will probably finish us, at any rate. For we shall find time only when the almond-tree flourishes and all the daughters of musick are brought low. But the time to write is now, when the day is full of engagements with interesting things and people, when a spare hour is hard to come by, and so will be put to better use. For writing is only thinking saddled and bridled and ready for a good gallop.

Then there are the questions of order and proportion. With historical order it is difficult to make the important points stand out in their proper salience; with logical, it is often difficult to know which is the parent idea that should rule the others. Some people do best by constructing little essay-kins, collecting them, sorting them like a card index, and writing from that. Some have their general idea, and take its various topics in more haphazard order, making a clear verbal connection compensate for some looseness in the plan. By either

method art is most art when it conceals art. When we
have no order, when "we faren as he that dronke is as
a mous", we put the reader to sleep:

> A dronken man wot wel he hath an hous,
> But he ne wot which is the right way thider,
> And to a dronken man the way is slider.

Right proportion is a part of order. The different topics
are of different sizes, of course, and it is important
to get each to its right size. The way is to be quite sure
what it is we are talking about at the moment. Rambling
is one error, and another is the purple patch. In a year's
time, when we re-read, it will nauseate us; but it will
not take a year for it to disgust the reader.

It was said by Aristotle and has been repeated by others
that a work of art should have a beginning, middle and
end. To that, later aesthetic seems to have added that
we should not be made too violently conscious that it
has them. The century that lay between the sonata
of Beethoven which began on a six-five chord and the
symphony of Vaughan Williams which ended on a
six-three has gradually made us less in love with exordium
and peroration. Quiet endings have been the fashion
since Victor Hugo's "Il n'était plus que la mer"—a fine
one, if he had not engineered it so carefully. The change
is due not so much perhaps to our being more modest
than our ancestors as to the gradual realization that
human effort, which includes writing articles, cannot
be final, and that there is something incongruous in giving
it a formal close; and that, again, is not unconnected
with the turn of the kaleidoscope from classic to romantic,
which we all feel but cannot define.

So at last the article is written; and now . . . "The Editor regrets". Who that writes has not received those words? The foolish think they close a door of condemnation; the wise know they open a window of hope. Something was wrong, and we are not told what; it is our business to find out. We are not told, chiefly because no one can tell us without spending much time. It may have been merely that the subject was not wanted just then, or that another article on that subject had anticipated it. It is not necessary to fear the worst, that the English is bad or the tone vulgar. It has been said that every article can be summarized in a paragraph, and every paragraph condensed into a sentence; and it may well be that, in some way or other, this particular article did not hold enough to the square inch. But by far the commonest reason for the *Kamschatka Evening News* having rejected an article is that the writer evidently does not know Kamschatka, or what sort of evenings they have there, or what would be news to them; or —worst of all—has not himself been a constant reader of the *Kamschatka Evening News*.

ORIENTAL

ANCIENT GREECE
(MARCH 1934)

G REEK music is the "Torquemada" crossword of classical studies. No one has any real hope of solving the puzzles it presents; no one who has the requisite knowledge of the facts can refrain from trying. Also just as a solution of a crossword does not bring an increased knowledge or appreciation of literature, so a working explanation of the dozen extant fragments is unlikely to bring either increased knowledge of Greek music or increased appreciation of music in general. The question will come to the front again shortly in a lecture by Mr. E. Clements to the Society for the Promotion of Hellenic Studies, Sir Henry Hadow being in the chair, and a whip having gone out to those who are likely to be able to contribute to the discussion.

The scholar's point of view differs from the musician's. Plato and Aristotle have said enough about the general character of the music to make us think the Greeks took it seriously, but being philosophers rather than artists they have left us in comparative ignorance of its actual nature. The one chorus of Euripides which

7

belongs to their time is too fragmentary to base anything
upon; the one treatise which describes the music they
may have heard leaves much unanswered. The scholar,
therefore, who knows a good deal about what the
Greeks accomplished in the other four fine arts is non-
plussed with regard to the music of that date. More is
known about the music of five centuries later, but that
is of considerably less interest to him, even if it gave,
which it does not, a clear idea of how that music actually
sounded in performance.

The musician, to whom music is first of all music,
and only secondly an element in a given civilization,
is not much moved either by the attitude of the philosophers, which is mainly mythological, nor by the deter-
minations of the treatises, which are mainly acoustical.
He wants to hear the music and judge for himself, to
learn about the instruments on which it was made,
where they came from, and how they were tuned,
whether concerted, whether in harmony, and what
prestige each had. He cannot begin to hear the music
of the Greeks until he knows what their conceptions
of time and tune were, and it is just on those that the
fragments and the treatises throw so little real light.
For the *time*, the three guesses—they can hardly be called
more—are that the music followed the poetical scansion
(a thing it does consistently nowhere else), that long
syllables connoted an agogic accent (which is possible),
and that the accents marked on the words implied varying
musical stresses (which comes up against another theory
of those accents). For the *tune*, there is fairly complete
evidence, but it is open to more than one interpretation.
And there are three specific elements—the drone,

grace notes, and percussion—of which nothing is known, without which, however, melodic music could hardly exist. Even if such questions as these were answered, it would still be necessary to have many more examples of the actual practice than are now at all likely to be found.

In despair of making anything at all satisfactory out of the fragmentary and undated examples which have come down to us, the musician will turn to modern Greek folk-song, of which there are collections of some hundreds. There he will see at least what the present-day Greek considers to be music. For though individual songs may travel all over the world and be considerably altered in the process, the country itself seldom changes its style. If he examines the collection of Pachtikos, which covers the region from Macedonia, through Hellas and the islands, to Cappadocia, he will come, perhaps, to some such conclusions as these: (1) that though the melody often begins with bold leaps, the main course of it is by step; (2) that the main contrast is between one-note-to-one-syllable and a melisma, in fact, between sedateness and scurry; (3) that the syllable bearing the verbal accent is set not to a high, but to a stressed note, and quantity has no influence on the time; and (4) that in a large minority of the songs the contrast of a diatonic and a chromatic section is felt, and desired in the same sort of way as we desire a contrast of major and minor. With these points in mind he may be inclined to think that the *Invocation to Calliope*, the *Epitaph of Seikilos* and the first Delphic Hymn are truly Greek tunes, and that the Hymns to the Sun and to Nemesis are probably not.

After the scholar and the musician there is another

who may be interested in this investigation. He is the
comparative ethnologist. It is to him that any facts about
the instruments would be useful, for they are precise.
The voice makes its own note subject to the feelings of
the moment; the note of the instrument is made beforehand, and the players' feelings do little to alter its pitch.
We know the scale of the Chinese *K'in* from 600 B.C.;
it was arrived at by taking strict aliquot parts of the
string. We know the scale of the Arabian *'Ud* (A.D. 700),
which was made by measuring off distances on the
string; and of the Indian *Vina* (A.D. 300), in which
both methods were employed. There are signs in both
the theory and the practice of the two latter countries
that Greek music was not unknown to them, and in the
second century Greek sculpture affected Indian. Will the
explorations at Cyprus throw any light on the cultural
relations of these different peoples? That the Chaldeans
tuned their harp by fifths becomes of greater interest now
that the early Aryans have had their provenance shifted
from Siberia to the Euphrates. Where Greece belonged
in all this tangle is a legitimate subject of enquiry.

(*Six weeks later*) . . . Mr. Clements shows by an
analysis of the six original Tonoi that one definite
tetrachord was implied in them all. This (putting *m*
for major tone, *n* for minor tone, and *s* for semi-tone)
was, for instance,

$$E \; s \; F \; n \; G \; m \; A$$

As a development of this came later another

$$E \; s \; F \; m \; G \; n \; A$$

which is the same as our "just" scale

$$B \; s \; |C \; m \; D \; n \; E \; s \; F| \text{ etc.}$$

From these two comes the intonation of all the modes, which differ in their distribution of *m*, *n*, and *s*. This point has not been noticed before, because the treatises draw no distinction between *m* and *n*, but call both of them *m*. It may be noted in passing that these intervals are also at the base of Indian music, and were, of course, embodied in the Church modes.

Now the one thing that is made clear by every one, from Plato to Luther, who has written of the modes that were current in his day, is that each mode had a character of its own which could be felt, and which we, who live in another day, do not feel: one was contemplative, another martial, a third playful, and so on. We accept these attributions, but with a literary rather than a musical faith, secretly wondering how the alteration of a semitone in the scale could affect its whole character in this way. And the reason we do not truly feel these distinctions is that we sing a mode as we speak a foreign tongue; and as we do not catch the subtle shades of meaning that underlie the words in our own vernacular, so in the music we miss the fine distinctions of mode which come out as minute stresses, glozings, graces, lingerings brought about by the new allegiance to another keynote. The mode, in fact, is much more than a change in the order of tone and semitone; there is more for us to hear, if we could hear it. How are we to do that?

Mr. Clements is clear on the subject. As a substitute for the long *melodic usedness* of the Greeks we must invent a *harmonic conviction* of our own. It is possible, in the light of a passage of Plutarch, of the Anonymus, and others to think that the Greeks had two-part harmony.

When we reflect on the centuries it took to establish
the principles of polyphony, we may be morally certain
that the Greeks had nothing at all like Mr. Clements's
facile counterpoint. But it does not matter. They had no
need of harmony or counterpoint: their mode was
perfectly clear to them without either. This harmonization is not for them but for us, who without its support
would at every moment lose hold of the mode, which is
vital. The harmonization then is frankly suppositious,
but it is perfectly strict; it employs no note that is not
in the mode as it has been established by him. If anyone
is purist enough to think that the harmony is un-Greek,
he can do without it; the mode will remain intact, but
he will not then taste it.

Mr. Clements's system, which can only be displayed
in technical language, rests entirely on inference from
that part of Alypius's notation in which we are sure the
system of Pythagoras is embodied. If the inference is
correct, then we have here the system of the best period.
It makes little use of the treatises which are mostly later,
but contains nothing that clashes with them. It is simple
and intelligible to us, but that cuts both ways; for we
may be quite sure that whatever their music may have
sounded like, it would not have sounded like ours. On
the other hand, it is musical sense, and all that the scholars
and acousticians have as yet provided us with is musical
nonsense. One thing is certain, that the Greeks had no
equal temperament, and these harmonies therefore sound
purer than ours: that in itself is sufficiently unlike our
music to be, possibly, like theirs. At any rate, if we are
looking for a music which can reasonably have belonged
to a people that fitted its plays with choric songs in open-

air theatres, that practised chamber music in its smaller
concert-room (*odeion*) and that made a name for itself
as a dancing nation, we may be sure that musical sense
has much more chance of being Greek than musical
nonsense.

INDIAN FOLKSONG

THERE are at present to be heard, if we will, some
Cingalese folksongs from Suriya Sena, assisted
by Nelun Devi (his wife). It is an opportunity of getting
hold of Indian music by the right end, and a better
chance for those who cannot go to the country—and
even for those who can—is not likely to recur. For most
of the musicians who have come over here have sung
and played us their art-music, the ripe fruit of many
centuries of melody-making; and in our inability to
make head or tail of conventions widely different from
our own, we have soothed ourselves with such fragments
of wisdom as "it is all in the minor mode", and "they
use quartertones, of course", as if that explained anything,
even if it were true. But these are actual folksongs,
gathered in the best possible way. Mr. Sena did not note
them down and leave them like dried flowers in an album.
Nor did he toil round with a couple of phonographs,
snap-shotting all and sundry, and when he had got them
home laboriously plot them on paper. He found a man
who knew a great many, stayed with him a long time,
and learned, by close imitation, to sing them in the same

way. Not only, then, are they the simplest form of Indian
song, but they are absolutely authentic.

As to the Indian conception of melody, let us take
those two heresies first. Indian music is not in "the"
minor; it is, roughly, in fifty minors *and* fifty majors—
enthusiasts say a thousand of each—but the point is
that in everything, pictures, temples, enamel, language
—everything, they love detail rather than structure.
After all, fifty and fifty is only a largish extension of the
three minors and two majors that our own folksong
knows, and they give the same general feeling to the
song. When people hear of twenty-two "quartertones"
they imagine they are all available for the same song;
but only seven of them are, as with us: once you have
heard clearly *which* seven, the song has no more notes
in it than ours. What do puzzle our ear are the grace-
notes; we seldom hear a clean, single note; without
being, or seeming, out of tune it seems to be always
embracing something of the note above or the note
below. That, and the queer leaps to a distant note,
not at all the ones we expect, make it difficult for us to
feel the beginning, middle, and end of anything.

This music, which is all melody, ought to be the very
thing for those who tell us that what they want in music
is "tune". They say "tune" because they don't know
what else to call it; but what they really mean is intelli-
gibility. There is plenty of evidence that Mozart seemed
tuneless to 1790 and Beethoven to 1830; but no one
now complains that the *Jupiter* or the *Fifth Symphony*
have no tune: to us they are all tune. But it is tune based
on the harmony. We pass easily from C to D, not because
it is the next note, but because there is a G lurking

somewhere down below which combines with either
and so mediates between them and keeps them in tune.
We get so familiar with C-D that we can sing or whistle
it without accompaniment (i.e., without a heard G).
Now the Indians go from C to D quite as often as we do,
but they do so *on another mediator* (the particular one
varies); so that our sense of C-D falsifies theirs, and
vice versa. Carry out that in imagination through a
thousand other, and more intricate, relationships, and
you see what it means to Europeanize an Indian tune, a
very easy and quite fatal thing to do. So, to the people
who ask for tune, we can say—Here it is, but you must
trust yourself completely to it and let it carry you
where it will, and not try to prophesy, as we often can
and do with our own tunes, where it is going.

Now the beauty of folksong all over the world is that
it has none of these intricate relationships, because it has
no mediators of any kind. In a folksong, we sail just as
comfortably as before from C to D, but we do it not from
any internal fitness, but because we have always heard
our mother and grandmother sing it so. We have
learnt it, and they learned it, as part of a phrase; and
having no mediator (i.e., no sense of implicit harmony)
they regard different D's as equally "in tune" with C.
Their scale is not like ours, a series of seven notes, but
a collection of little phrases fitting together as best they
may between two C's. I had an instance of this in the
jungle. I wanted to know the series of notes on a pipe.
My interpreter understood what was wanted, but no
words of his could explain to the boy a thing that was
quite outside his experience: he merely continued his
quirks and twirls as before, until I took his fingers one

by one and lifted them off the holes. He probably thought
me quite unmusical.

With all these difficulties before us, it is comforting
to find that Mr. Sena makes our approach as easy as
possible. Indians, and most non-European peoples, sing
in a nasal voice, probably because that is the line of least
resistance. (We noticed the same with the Vatican choir
when they were here some years ago. They have to fill
a large space, and often; and they economize energy by
dropping into this nasal tone.) Such a tone makes the
Indian song still more difficult to understand and *feel*:
the voice we are accustomed to "explains" things best,
just as a tune is easier to make out on the piano, which is
familiar, than on the bagpipe or ukulele. Mr. Sena in
the first place speaks English perfectly, having been
at Tonbridge and St. John's, Cambridge, and, in the
second, sings as one of Clive Carey's pupils would sing.
It is wonderful how with this voice the song comes out
of the twilight into broad day. I am not speaking without
book: I heard two, and one of them moved me, as once
before did an Ernakulam boatman, and a Tanjore school-
mistress, and a Kanika of Trivandrum. But I am not going
to tell you any more about him: you must go and hear
him for yourself.

Those who think, and sometimes tell us, that extra-
European music is a side-issue, have only part of the
truth. Some day we shall have an aesthetic which will
show us what music is really doing in the world; at
present we merely know that, whatever it does, we want
it to go on doing that. And whatever that may be,
Indian music does it no whit less than European. Our
harmony supplies to a melody both wealth and orienta-

tion: Indian music has none, but its grace notes serve precisely those two purposes, and without them they feel the melody to be both thin and indefinite. Our counterpoint carries on the interest over the dead points: their drumming does the same. Our orchestration combines tone-qualities: they prefer them single, as we did up to Handel's time. The human needs are fundamentally the same. Their music has its own beauty, which is not ours; but it is no more a side-issue than the Greek anthology, or Homer, or the book of Genesis.

FOLKSONG

PAN

MACHINES do this for us: they show how important the man is behind them. We never knew till the gramophone came how flawless we wanted our music to be. No one who can get a good record will buy a bad one, so the standard rises imperceptibly day by day. There is a class of singer which can record and one which cannot, and the latter need not apply. Wireless, again, brings the sound close to the ear, and every virtue and defect of a voice is magnified, so that vocalization, which is labour and skill, rises in value, and there is no market for the dozen things that constitute charm, which is a gift. The voice responds quickly to example, and we may expect the process to breed, as time goes on, the flawless, soulless voice; in fact we hear it now.

The machine standardizes; it also multiplies copies. We can hear a symphony, or a single bar of it, ten times running if we please; and we can have a concert of the sort we like at least once a day, as against, say, a couple of dozen times a year, as it used to be. We get our music literature, as we may call it, sitting in a room with well-stocked shelves and with a good and instantaneous

18

service of a circulating library. With practical perfection and ample choice we ought soon to know all the music worth knowing. It is already a drawing-room game to compete in whistling from memory the themes of the *Wohltemperirtes* and of Beethoven's nine scherzos; our children will get out their stave-ruled pocketbooks in the Tube to solve Torquemada II's diagram of crochets and quavers.

But in all this there is a catch somewhere. It can be put in a sentence. *No one understands a thing properly unless he does it with his own hands.* Sailing in over the Exmouth bar in a four-ton boat is exciting, but to do it holding the sheet in one hand and the tiller in the other is life itself. When one does a thing with one's own hands perfection is usually unattainable and choice is limited; but presently both are seen to be unnecessary. The essential glory of the thing lies in the trying and the gradually getting better at it; success would only mean that we must now crack some other nut. All the perfection and scope of machinery puts us no nearer that particular glory, and so great is the pleasure it gives that a large part of mankind has tacitly held that such virtue ought to be its own reward, even if it has tempered that view in practice by a somewhat capricious remuneration.

When Pan called to Syrinx in the river-bed, he was composer, performer, and sole listener. We have in course of time thought it better to break up that unity into a trinity, and to specialize; but Nature will not be driven out with a fork. When a composer cannot play what he writes he is apt to be as little convincing as the man who reads out his speech because he daren't talk it. When a conductor, who in any case plays by proxy, cannot compose on emergency, he is little better off than a shipbuilder who has not been through the workshop, and a listener, who has never stumbled through accompaniments and spoilt a few sheets or quires of music paper, makes little of any song he hears for the first time, and even less of the singer unless he himself is one. Those who "know what they like" without having tried what they can do are the prey of every whim, unless they are the blind followers of the latest authoritative pronouncement.

But is Pan quite dead? Even in a literal sense, we have read somewhere lately that he holds meetings of a "Pipers' Guild", which makes mellow noises till the thrushes come thronging to enquire what is toward. "I do wish", writes one of these human thrushes,

> there was some way of conveying the sound of a pipe by letter . . . Primitive music on a primitive instrument is most enlightening, and I have already untrained my ear from the modern diatonic scales in a way I never hoped to. We did lose a lot by developing keyboard instruments like the piano. . . . The language may be quite unintelligible, and perhaps one may never be able to learn it, but what it is trying to express is the innermost self of the player with no ulterior motive to obscure it . . . How odd and how very good it is that a piece of bamboo can transport one so quite away from the otherwise mouldy present.

Wireless has made the voice of the Kent nightingale known to all the other counties, but after the initial wonder of that we want something deeper. When Beethoven after the twittering and rustling and purling of the *Scene am Bach* produces an actual nightingale we are secretly a little disappointed; he was saying in delicious metaphor how good it is to be quit of "the otherwise mouldy present", and now he seems merely to transfer us from one present to another, even if a better one. It is art we want, not Nature, but a simpler art, and more direct than machinery can give, one we can take part in ourselves. In London alone there are hundreds of houses where a string quartet meets, and thousands filled with chamber music. Nobody hears them: they are easily lost in the din of the street gramophone with the megaphone attachment, whose proprietor neither gets not gives pleasure. But they are too busy "expressing the innermost self of the player" to want to be heard. They are their own listeners, sometimes one of them is the composer as well, and they are laying a gift on an altar.

> White Daphnis, he who pipes so clear
> The songs our shepherds love to hear,
> Offers to Pan these little wares,
> Pierced reeds, a stick to throw at hares,
> Sharp hunting-spear and brown fawnskin,
> And scrip he carried apples in.

THE WILTSHIRE FESTIVAL

I STOLE away last week from opera and civilization— and incidentally, I suppose, from my duty—because I wanted to go and hear the nightingale throbbing and bubbling in the high wood, and the cuckoo shredding in his counterpoint below in the valley of the Wylie. For if there is one thing certain in the world of music, where everything is as uncertain as words can make it, it is that nothing whatever is to be got out of listening to what you are not in the mood for. To be in the mood for it—to "take his intent", as R. B. calls it— is your only wisdom. Music is like the Psalms in that respect; we have heard these often enough to take them for granted and to give them but little attention, till "something happens", when the time-worn sentences spring to life; they are as if written for this very happening.

It is so, too, with "those small folk-songs" of the birds that they hand on from father to son, as another R. B. tells us, "unchanging to the changeful generations of men". So, too, with our human folksongs. The young people turn away from them to something topical or exciting—just now, to jazz; those in the prime of life, who are busy with the advancement of the art, pass them by as too elementary, or as a pose; and the old, who know and love them, hide them out of sight and hearing, for fear of anyone trampling on their feelings by laughing at what they prize. And so folksong and folk-like song does not come by its rights till something happens. What happened on this occasion was that seven hundred children sang them as one. These boys and girls had come in from Salisbury and Wilton, Chippenham and Corsham, Swindon and Wootton Bassett, to Devizes, the hub of the wheel. They had started soon after dawn, the girls in white frocks, the boys in minus fours, by car and bus; and here they were with their lunch in their pockets ready to sing all day, and then trundle home to bed with the happy, tired feeling of something attempted, something done.

We examined them first. Mr. Plunket Greene, a kind of *genius loci*, dragged them out of themselves, singing and acting for their benefit both the right and the wrong way; Mr. Clive Carey packed much good advice in small parcels; Mr. Wiseman, from Edinburgh, put an unerring finger on the point for praise or blame; and Miss Sybil Eaton, from Rutland, let nothing go by default and afterwards practised what she preached. Three or four hours of it—quite an easy day—ten or twelve is not unknown. Then came the rehearsal, and the concert, conducted by Mr. Carey, who made irresistible faces and sang still more irresistible songs, and Mr. Wiseman who did what he liked with them; and one of the things he liked was for the children to teach the audience how to sing *The Jolly Waggoner*. They did, and as we had done not so badly they gave us a spontaneous round of applause. The first class sang more exalted things, such as Howells's by no means obvious *The Tinker's Song* and Vaughan Williams's *Sound Sleep*; and an efficient string orchestra (all local, led by Miss Eaton) filled in gaps with Bach and Gordon Jacob.

These children were happy: you could not mistake their faces, or their swaying bodies, or their tightening hands and arms, or their eyes that said "Command me anything! *What* can I do for you?" to the man with the stick. And, of course, it means very little to that music which grown-ups like to have made for them that a few hundreds of Wiltshire boys and girls should be perfectly happy for a day making it; or that Wiltshire labourers should screw to save the necessary half-crown,

and get up at four to milk the cows so as to see their
children off, and arrange for someone to milk in the
evening so that they may see them safely home; or that
devoted schoolmistresses should toil for weeks (often
quite on the wrong lines, bless them, but, with luck,
better next time), getting the little monkeys to attend
and to believe there may be something in it, and then
having their hopes dashed by defeat and going boldly
at it again next year. But it is not a small thing to the
children or their mothers, who after darning and mending
them come and sing too, nor was it to the Cumberland
folk where Mary Wakefield started it, nor to the Cornish
when Lady Mary Trefusis was alive, nor to the Dorking
people where Dr. Vaughan Williams thinks it worth
while to toss aside the MS. of his new opera and come
and lend a hand, nor to scores of places throughout
England and English-speaking countries.

"A stunt", say some; "you are merely engineering
enthusiasm through a countryside that only wants to
be let alone." Not at all: each new festival that is started
is like the smiting of the rock in Horeb; the stream of
music comes bubbling up from the cavity where it has
long waited for this outlet. And then, if the wisdom of
this age has driven from the land the squires and their
sons who used to captain (and subsidize) the village
cricket team, must it not find some new social interest
in order to justify itself? "And competition!" say others;
"Isn't music an end in itself? Does it need to be bolstered
up by competition?" Bluntly, yes; it does. Cricket
and football are none the worse for county matches and
cup-ties, so long as they don't become too professional.
These festivals are run by amateurs under professional

guidance, and the villages compete just as they did in the madrigal time (when, incidentally, cross-country football was in vogue).

And now, when I get back to duty, I find awaiting me Mr. Gerald Abraham's *This Modern Stuff*. He shows us how the harmonies we dread are only doing what harmony has always done—short-circuiting the lines of its predecessors; how melody is, as Donald Tovey long ago called it, the surface of those harmonies, and therefore necessarily just as dreadful; and how this generation has made a corner in rhythm—jazz, if nothing better—it being the way of generations to explore one thing at a time. It all seems very sound; and yet we feel such matters to belong to the brain, whereas folksong, ornithological or human, is clearly an affair of the heart. Well, there may be room for both.

OPERA

EARLY OPERA

THE story of early opera has often been told, at least as history books can tell it. It amounts to little more than a string of names, dates, and anecdotes, the sort of thing that every well-informed person ought to know, and that leaves the ill informed gasping for air. The right way to know the truth about opera is to be in it, whether as conductor or call-boy; short of that, one—the writer of this article included—to some extent beats air. Still, when Mr. Robert Stuart takes the trouble to give a three-week season of early opera the dates being (for the well informed), *Orpheus*, 1607—*Cupid and Death*, 1659—*Dido and Aeneas*, 1689—*Julius Caesar*, 1723—*Alcestis*, 1767—*La Finta Giardiniera*, 1774—*Freischütz*, 1820—an article of some sort is called for, if only as a gesture of welcome.

And, now that you look at the list, doesn't your mouth water? And isn't there just a passing pang that you didn't hear the first three of the series—for, you know, you didn't come in any large numbers, although, theoretically, it is of interest to you to understand how a form of art which the public voice places at the head of all musical effort behaved in swaddling clothes.

Confining ourselves to the two operas and one masque we have heard—because until we actually hear it music does not exist for most of it—we see that they are three entirely different things; and that, incidentally, may warn us not to be too ready to generalize about opera. What is usually done is to fix upon some one opera as a standard—nowadays the *Meistersinger*, formerly *Don Giovanni*, and earlier still Gluck's *Orfée*—and praise each competitor as he approaches this. "Men are bad", they say, with Aristotle, "in many ways, but good in only one". Yet of operas, and perhaps of other phenomena, it would be truer to say that there is a fair sprinkling of bad saints and good villains, and that there is no one way at all. Monteverde, for instance, did the unexpected. Born when Palestrina was in his prime, there was every reason why he should die a famous madrigalist. Instead of which, as the judge said, he went fiddling about with regals (harmoniums) and gravicembani (harpsichords of a kind), besides the viol which he could himself play, thinking how he could import them into music, which then only meant singing. (We find it difficult to understand his problem, because to us music is chiefly instruments, and we are beginning to wonder what to do with the voice.) The voice had never yet, in serious music, sung alone—it had always repeated its words and tune, even many times, and it was tied and bound with a chain of polyphonic figures and phrases; and to anyone who knows his cinquecentists a dozen pages of *Orpheus* look like Stephenson's "Rocket" (replacing the colliery engine) and its carriages (half-fledged stage-coaches). He set the voice free. That was a small matter: he was merely laughed at for it, as an illiterate; any peasant on the banks of the Ticino could do as much. His real problem was *how to go on*. The madrigals had done it automatically; one voice had led in the next, before it had time to get into difficulties with its own tune. Now that the next was no longer there to be led in, it floundered and repeated itself after half a dozen bars.

We are not told which of the two composers really wrote *Cupid and Death*, and which looked on. If Locke wrote it he cannot have written the "*Macbeth* music" thirteen years later, is all that we can say. A tune can now stand on its own legs, though its stride is short. It can "close" where it wants to, instead of having to fly to any port in a storm. It still hugs the land, like mariners before the invention of the compass (key). In essence it is not much more than the galliard and pavan (three and four time) of Bull and Byrd, but it has acquired certain facilities and amenities which make it decidedly more presentable. The dances and intermezzi are the cream of the thing; one hears in them the steps of the morris and the figures of the country-dance, and, with that, a certain sincerity. The songs lack grip, just as Shirley's words do; and *Cupid and Death* has at least the operatic virtue of fitting music to words. Yet a masque is not an opera; it leads, in fact, in the opposite direction. Its appeal is to the cultured classes, primarily, since it personifies the passions instead of presenting them in drama; yet its "turns" rely on sheer skill, like those of the music-hall, and are only redeemed from that by the unity of the plot. It is, in fact, essentially a "show", enhanced by apposite words and incidental music. But that *tertium quid* which opera aims at and sometimes achieves, that something which is neither in words nor in tune, but results from both, is not within its scope.

The world has agreed to call Purcell's *Dido and Aeneas* a work of genius; and it is certainly the most conspicuous work of musical genius England has produced, unless we admit the claim made for him to be an Irishman. We are mostly content to hold this belief as an act of faith, but there must have been some in the theatre who held it on conviction. For what Handel did to Muffat, what Mozart did with Attwood's exercises, and what Korsakov failed to do for Moussorgsky, that Purcell does with the work of his contemporaries; and this strikes more forcibly when they are heard in close succession. It is not the ingenious canons and ground basses and typically musical devices that fill these pages, for they are so naturally introduced that we hardly notice them till we look afterwards to see what it was that we heard. It is the leverage that one moment gets on the next, the driving force, the rightness of the structural lines, the thinking not in bars but in pages, and going straight for the things that matter. And over it all there is a freshness and a sparkle, and a masterfulness. For instance, in the famous echo. Echo repeats sometimes the last two words, sometimes more. That point is got. But it always repeats *totidem verbis*, and nine men out of ten would have made it do so; Purcell, however, makes it change its harmonies, a most unecho-like proceeding, because he is not imitating Nature, but telling us, as a good landscape-painter does, what it is that he particularly likes in it; and that is not its inevitability but its suggestion. And with it all there is nothing that Mr. Josiah Priest's young ladies could not reasonably hope to dance or sing; and the violins are in easy keys and the first position.

Above all, *Dido* is short (it plays barely an hour), and, what is more, it seems short, whereas both *Orpheus* and *Cupid* seem long. It may be worth considering whether operas in general are not too much cut to one length; one cannot help thinking that the prolixities of *Tristan* and *Walküre* and some arid tracts in *Rosenkavalier* are there to "fill an evening". An opera lasts just as long as it holds us in thrall. After that we want to get to bed.

A HOME OF OPERA
(FEBRUARY 1932)

THE news that Covent Garden has definitely abandoned the idea of a season of international opera for this year, coupled with the fact that they have been engaged in the suburbs of London for some weeks past in the performance of opera in English by Englishmen, is welcome, and may prove to be a turning-point. It is possible that experience has shown them the true interpretation of the old phrase—*qui facit per alium facit per se*, and that it may really mean—"if you want a thing done properly, do it yourself". When we were rich we bought opera abroad; now we are poor, we must make it ourselves or go without it. With that turn of fortune's wheel may come the reflection that it would have been better if we had made it without waiting for necessity.

It would have been better in this way. Whether we like it or not, the course of history shows that there is no centre for the music of a State other than the Church or the opera. We sometimes lament over—shall we say, whine about?—the state of music here. Some have lately asked that it shall be "protected"; but that, as a merely negative proposal and as a confusion of issues, has fallen flat. We want something positive to work for, some goal to aim at, some standard to reach. Opera of our own, with life in it, would provide that. We know all the arguments against it: The English don't want opera (but they go to it, especially abroad); they want nothing short of the very best (but seldom get it); they don't want a thing that is neither drama nor music (that is what we say when either the singing or the acting has been below par, and forget about when either is good); "they never give the operas I want" (because you don't go often); drama falsifies music (that'll require a new paragraph); opera costs too much (the home-grown article will cost less).

Yes, drama falsifies, or, at least, disturbs or alters music. Applied music is to absolute music as a debate is to a speech; the pivots are quite different. What we call the "symphonic" passages of Wagner—the descent to the Rhine, the long waiting for Isolde—are not really "absolute"; the turmoil of thoughts in Brünnhilde's enlightened and Tristan's diseased brain calls the music continually off its true line; its steady flame flares up and dies down in response to gusts of passion extraneous in it. In Mozart's age, with everything in water-tight compartments, the problem of development hardly arose; the cavatina or scena made a triptych by itself. In post-

Wagnerian opera—*Sadko* or *Wozzeck* or, especially,
Pelléas—the music is kept at such an unobtrusive level
that if it did develop no one would notice the fact. All
this worries or bores the pure musician; he does not wish
to be "called off". Well, he need not go and hear it; but
his common sense will tell him two things. First, that
knowing the deep passion his own music inspires in
him, and what a pleasure it is to find others sympathizing
with what means so much to him, it is only fair that he
should reciprocate, and wish well to an enterprise that
appeals deeply to other musical minds. But secondly,
if opera does really act as the flywheel of a country's
music he will benefit too, indirectly but really. The more
music is in the air, talked, thought, written about,
competed in, the more the standard rises; and his own
choral society, chamber music, orchestra will get a
fillip from the fact that an opera directly employs, for
weeks or months of rehearsal, from one to two hundred
people in a business in which they, at least, heartily believe.

But they must be our own people. The employment
of the best artists from abroad will not make a pin's
head of difference to our own music. It is sometimes
said we shall profit by their example. That is just solemn
nonsense. No one ever learned anything yet by looking
on: he must do it himself, there is no other way; though,
while he is doing that, there is no harm in his going occasionally to see how it is better done. Now how is he to
do it? Of the five operas that we have, or have lately had,
in London there is one that will just suit him. As against
the touring of the Carl Rosa it lives and works in its
own home; as against the republic of the B.N.O.C.
it lives and moves under a tyranny; as against the

endowments of Covent Garden and Beecham opera, it lives and thrives on a debt. The debt of the Vic-Wells did not come from extravagance: it was a bit of wise and daring policy. The tyranny is really a constitutional monarchy; there is an energetic governing body. The home is the thing, and what that brings—tradition, a tradition of 114 years. Born the Royal Coburg, rechristened the Royal Victoria, it took to music, but unluckily also to drink and disorder. The large-hearted Emma Cons reclaimed the wastrel, calling it the Royal Victoria Coffee Hall. It began in the new century to sing operatic selections, with tableaux, collected a chorus, and with the war gave complete operas and Shakespeare plays. Two years ago it annexed Sadler's Wells, with the right prestige, the right locale, and cheap at the price. We may well call it the "old" Vic: it has a past.

Pay off its debt (under £30,000) and give it a working income (say, £3,000) and in ten years' time you will have opera there to which you will be glad to take your friends. It began at the beginning, the only sensible way, and in eighteen years it has learnt a good deal about opera. It knows that the audience must understand what it is seeing and hearing, so it has only English, and gets it pronounced. It knows that formality is forbidding and high prices prohibitive. It somehow conveys to the gallery that they are part of the thing (one of them looked down on some empty stalls one night when she was enjoying herself mightily. "What a shime!" she said, and collecting 240 pennies from her factory, put them in a bag and gave them to Miss Baylis). It knows that the music colleges are only too glad to find openings for their students, and a surprising number of these are

D

grateful enough to come back when they have made their name and sing for nominal fees. It knows that people have old associations they like to revive, and curiosity they like to satisfy, and it neglects neither class. To go there is like going home.

In ten years you will have opera, and in twenty you will have a home of opera, a school where all operatically minded English men and women will go for the certificate that will push them off into life. Towards the mid-century people will be wondering why we took so long about doing the obvious thing, which was to make the foundation secure on which English opera could flourish in the magnificence of Covent Garden, the enterprise and wit of Beecham, and the courage and endurance of the Carl Rosa. Besides a school for singers and a foundation for other effort, it will be a trying-out ground where the intelligent student will be able to see at first hand, not merely by his history books, why there must be so many failures for one success in a work which asks every musical resource a man possesses, and the experienced composer to check and prune and shape his invention against the blunt human facts.

AN IMPRESARIO

OPERA is the question of the week, as it has been of so many weeks in the past. The management of opera is an exceptionally thorny question. It is as difficult, though on a smaller scale, as governing a State, and for similar reasons. In both there are a number of perfectly sincere people of divergent views thinking, and trying to think, what is for the ultimate good of the governed: in both there is another number of people thinking how to further their own interests in the conditions which the former establish. In the operatic world there are, in fact, statesmen and politicians. What we do in the political world is to put a Prime Minister at the head to reconcile divergent opinion and eventually get something done that is worth doing.

What the operatic world needs is, similarly, a prime minister. He is usually called an impresario. We had one once. His name was Augustus Harris. He made mistakes, as we all do, but he had an eye and an ear, and he used them. Put a row of singers in front of him, and he would tell you which of them was any good for the purpose of opera. Bring him to see three or four ballets, and he would say which one would please. He gauged his audience and knew instinctively which of two actors would suit their taste, and which would suit some other audience. Even the abstruse art of conducting did not puzzle him. Like King Edward VII, who accorded him his friendship, he knew a *man* when he saw one, and he weighed the advice of those he could trust as to his musicianship; for musicians are many, but men with a real personality are few.

Yet this question of an impresario, so vital, one would have thought, so primary in other walks of life, where he is called an archbishop, a Lord Chancellor, an admiral, a headmaster, and so on, has not been even mentioned in the communications to the Press which we have read this week. Instead of that, we have heard something about three other questions—about finance, about a particular conductor, and about a particular company. As to finance, it is an ill business telling other people how to spend their money; but in so far as some of it is ours, we sincerely hope that through "Opera in English" and "English Opera", i.e., English in language and English in style, two very different stages, we may eventually found a tradition. That appears to be the root meaning of Lady Snowden's communication to the Press. The spirit behind it is a thing that leaves a glow in us. Here is a burning desire to help her compatriots, and no one in high place has before now thought seriously and persistently of helping music.

We may have our qualms about the way in which it is proposed to do that. It may seem to some that it is wrong, even iniquitous, to take public money and spend it on the foreigner, and the hint that there will have to be some foreign "stars" in the company amounts to that. Others may think it very doubtful whether the British Broadcasting Corporation, which at present appears to the world to be a congeries of diverse opinion, is at all fitted to be the nucleus of a ministry of Fine Arts. But we are still to have a further pronouncement as to the exact scheme which it is intended to adopt, and it would be premature now to discuss these points. "Whate'er is best administered is best." We were never so good at making schemes as in carrying them out. Whether it is to be by Lady Snowden's indomitable enthusiasm or Sir Thomas Beecham's tried skill and sure artistic judgment, or by some combination of these, the result will come about by doing, not by talking. For nothing is more certain about the vague art of music than this,

that it cannot be taught, and that it can only be caught
from some centre of infection.

It ought not to be difficult for Covent Garden to do
better in its next season than it did in its last, if it sets
about the task in time. It might seem an easy thing to
sing in English instead of in a foreign language, but in
fact it is a new problem. We can bear one actor with a
foreign accent, especially if he is Octave Dua, but the
bulk must be English actors, and they can only be trained
slowly. Three or four of them did quite well in their
novel situation, and if only the frame can be preserved
more figures will come forward to fill the picture. The
mistakes were those of the management. They misjudged
the state of the case. They were offering an inferior
article, and they asked too high a price. They had played
to the provinces at 5s. 9d. with success, and they thought
when they came to London and added the halo of Covent
Garden they might ask 15s.; but better opera was to be
had in London at that moment for 5s. As the whole
thing was an experiment, they thought they might
experiment with the conductor, and they put an untried
man to conduct *Parsifal*. As the audience was also new,
they ventured to treat its musical taste with contempt,
and they allowed a baritone to finish Figaro's air on a
high C.

All these are matters with which the right kind of
impresario would have no difficulty in dealing, or rather,
he would have difficulty, but would surmount it. He
would certainly know his public better than to ask
what they wouldn't pay, and then would gradually nurse
them into paying what they never thought they could.
He would have no experiments with conductors, and no

nonsense with baritones. He would go his own way, and not ask advice from outside, but would weigh the advice of experts on technical points. There would probably be some mistakes of taste until he knew better, and these he would have to balance with other positive attractions; there would be few real errors of judgment. They tell us we have few singers (I do not agree) and that the public will not come to hear singer or conductor with any but a foreign name. Continue, then, our excellent practice of adopting foreign names, and as soon as one of them establishes his fame, reveal the fact that he is English; the public will be openly cross and secretly pleased. Put the conductor behind a screen: it is wonderful how few know who is conducting, except by sight, and some amusement might be had out of this. For your true impresario will be, among other things, a man of humour.

DO WE WANT OPERA?

THE average English musician thinks he has settled the question by saying simply "I don't like opera." That may be very true, but it is neither here nor there. There was once an artillery Colonel, whose wife said to him on Sunday morning, at half-past ten, "My dear, I don't want to go to church"; to which he replied, "Of course, my dear, no one *wants* to go to church". It is that aspect of the matter that the musician might profitably consider—not whether he wants opera, but whether opera, and the whole cause of music behind it, does not want him; whether music does not depend upon singing, and good singing upon opera, and opera upon his allegiance. He is apt to think of opera as a fad of imperfect musicianship, and to picture a State subsidy or some millionaire as settling the matter without his help or his blessing. He does not see that his own musical prospects are intimately connected with the establishment and maintenance of native opera.

"CARMEN"

Two of the cast sang "Opera in English". The rest sang it in Jabberwocky. Let us leave . . .

ENGLISH PRONUNCIATION

Not a few of those who sit and listen wish to hear the words, but not too well. They think that some little mystery in them helps the atmosphere of the music. Or else, as Robert Bridges once confessed was his case, they prefer not to hear the words at all, because then they are not obliged to notice what a mess the music is making of them. They like Latin because there is an orotund sound about it, because it does not as a rule convey a story that one needs to know, and because if one has forgotten it, one will probably—and here they look round the room—not be alone in that. If people really wanted to understand, why was *Schwanda* (presumably written in Czech) sung last week in German, not in English? There was no question here of spoiling the phrases of the original language, as there is when Puccini is sung in French and Mozart in German; because we none of us know Czech. It was just the feeling that unless an opera is in a foreign tongue we are somehow not getting our money's worth.

WAGNER OPERAS

A PRINCIPAL rock of stumbling was the English translation. That, I take leave to say, is solemn humbug. One does not, in any opera, hear more than a fifth of the words, at a liberal estimate. No Englishman can get at the sense with two words of German out of ten; with two words of English he can, and does. Further, anyone who says that Jameson's translation is worse nonsense than the original convicts himself of not knowing enough German to distinguish meaning from bombast or prose from poetry. Thirdly, anyone who thinks that music must be sung in the original, because the composer fitted his music to it like a glove to the hand, shows that he has not had the opportunity of listening in to an opera with the score in front of him, in which case he would have seen how many singers, in the heat of action, take that glove off.

CONDUCTORS

THE BOW ON THE BATON

At mezzo, his coat, shirt, and collar were dripping,
At forte, the stick from his fingers was slipping;
But there's one I sat under I'll never forget—
The conductor was dry and the orchestra wet.

EMIL WAGNER

WHEN Richard Wagner wrote his paper *On Conducting* (published simultaneously in Leipzig and New York, 1869), violas were usually "infirm violinists or decrepit wind-players", a man was promoted "by seniority" to be conductor, critics "barked when their mouths were not stopped (which they usually were)", the conductors came to be "pianoforte pedagogues protected by ladies-in-waiting", and salvation came at last "from the virtuosi" upon different orchestral instruments. Wagner came, in fact, into a naughty world and (with the *Meistersinger* and three operas of his tetralogy behind him) as one born to set it right. Conducting was then a new art. It was not much more than a generation since Spohr had substituted the stick for the music-roll, and from that back to the time when

the first violin indicated with his bow a start or a change
of time was perhaps only one more. Wagner is concerned
chiefly to wake up a sleepy Germany and get them out
of their sloppy ways and tepid thinking. His invective
is pointed at the "worthy" Ferdinand Hiller and the
"elegant" Mendelssohn, pitting them against Liszt
and Bülow. Weingartner wrote in 1896 under the same
title, and to the same general effect, but calling Bülow
"didactic" and Siegfried Wagner a "tempo-rubato-
conductor". The main object of both books is to insist
that the conductor has two things to do: to choose and
maintain the right tempo, and to divine "the sense and
meaning in a complex of notes, the thread which holds
them together, the 'line' whose true observance suddenly
makes a trite work stand out as inevitable, and which is
its genius, its kernel." This Wagner called the "melos",
and his detractors revenged themselves by sneering at
his "eternal melody".

He foresaw the "stunt-conductor" under whom we
are sometimes called upon to suffer, and his namesake, a
member of the Munich orchestra whose little ditty we
have just read, points to one of such a conductor's
weaknesses; the "one I sat under" is Richard Strauss.
Now comes a book written by a member of the Berlin
opera orchestra (*Ein Orchester-musiker über das Diri-
gieren* by Hans Diestel, with a preface by Strauss) which
explains in some detail what are the sufferings of the
players. The style is not easy; he is a parenthetic gentleman, and the full-stop is sometimes so far off as to be
lost to view; but his sentences are generally worth
the trouble of unravelling, even when we burn with
desire to rewrite them. He enunciates two principles:

1. By means of the point of the stick time is to be translated into space. The movements are limited by the shape (which shows the time) and the size (which indicates the dynamics) of the beat-figures.

2. During the performance the work alone must form the connecting link between conductor and players. The conductor gives his whole attention to the work and to the task of inducing his men, by bracing their minds, to concentrate upon it. Any communication from him which, by way either of instruction or rebuke, ignores the work for the moment, is totally inadmissible.

The important matters are "the point of the stick" and "attention to the work in hand".

For the first of these he quotes Wagner: "I do not beat time; that would make the performance stiff. I paint it in the air." The stick is not a mere emblem of office, but a real instrument, as important as the bow is to the violinist. In unworthy hands it becomes a sort of "trailer" (*Anhängsel*) to the arms and lags behind the time. To lay it down and conduct with the hand, as is sometimes done, is to throw away a chief means of expression. To conduct with the hand and *not* to transmit the time to the point of the stick will do for the second violins; but then the left hand must be added for the firsts, and the drummer will in the meantime be bored by the tautology. When the beat figure is not performed by the stick (i.e., wrist and fingers) the arm is called in, and that tends to involve the body, and before long we may have treading or stamping the time, stooping at the knees, crouching and springing up, throwing the head about, fidgeting, jumping, whirling of the arms, opening the mouth, and the like. When the time does not travel through to the point, but remains in the hand which strikes and chops and lunges as if it were playing the piano, 1 becomes indistinguishable from 2, 2 from 3, because of the much smaller ambit of the beat-figure.

As to the management of the stick, the temptation has to be resisted to beat notes instead of time; the metrical values within the bar constitute a danger zone. An alla breve, or a common time which is beaten as such, is a difficult place; the key to it is a firm unadorned upbeat, which prepares the downbeat without hesitation. A change of beat (four to the bar, for instance, instead of two) should be entered upon not at the beginning of a rallentando but after it has begun, and it is seldom necessary at all. Once you disturb the player's concentration, tone and delivery (*Auftrag*) both suffer: the conductor must confine himself to movements that rivet attention. The smaller the average extent of the beat-figures, the greater will be the distinction, strength, and command of those which exceed or fall short of it. Angular or jerky movements of the stick have the evil result that the phrases fall apart, drag or hurry, and that the time is not picked up quickly because of the greater interval between the beats, and because the line is not made clear at once, but only after a series of such beats. The snapping off of a pause, or the beating out of a tremolando chord in recitative, are equally disturbing.

It is not unusual to let the left hand merely duplicate the right. Two things then happen. Any apposite indication it might give (such as a "piano" with the flat of the hand) is lost in the mass of meaningless gestures, and the conductor gets very hot. Liszt laughed at "the worthy Lords Privy Seal of the secret of conducting who usurp the function of windmills and seek in the sweat of their brow to convey to their men their incandescent inspiration." Directly the conducting is confined, however, to the point of the stick, we get rid of all this. The left hand, kept free, can hush down particular sections or players, help over difficulties or correct errors, quicken one part or check another, or touch the telegraphic time-beater (which, however, is not of much use except in syncopated passages) for a chorus in the wings. The only signs that are really necessary are those that show the time, the line, and the amount of tone, and that produce concentration. But we see a good many others—the stick poked at someone who has the melody, shot out for a 'cello lead (which they could have found for themselves), the fist clenched in the direction of the trumpet (who accordingly blares), abrupt glances here and there while the arms are thrown up (for more tone) or the body crouches (for less). Such signs are didactic or punitive; if the latter, since they do not say what the fault is nor what its correction would be, they are, if given in public, insulting. How much better Arthur Nikisch's plan! In a big work the second clarinet stopped playing, left out an important passage, and at last got in again. After the concert Nikisch said nothing. A year later when the work came on again he asked the artist why it was. A sheet had dropped out of his part.

There is much more in the book—what the audience and what the critics have said, the vexed question of uniform bowmarks for the violins (not the 'cellos, because the audience don't see them)—but this will give an idea of it. The book might well be translated. It will not help an audience; they had better shut their eyes and listen, since the stick will as often as not mean the wrong thing except to those who are actually wrestling with the work. To both bow and baton it is full of real help.

THE CONDUCTOR IN THE MAKING

MUSIC is born in the country and comes to the town. From Mons and Arras it journeyed to Rome, from Mannheim and Stuttgart to Frankfurt and Leipzig, from Indore, Lucknow, and Tanjore to the three great coast towns. We see it doing the same here. From the "Westcuntre" (which may mean the Welsh border) mentioned in a thirteenth-century book, and a Northumbria (including Yorkshire), it found a home in neighbouring abbeys. To judge from the birthplace of the madrigalists, which are seldom west of the Pennines, its home in the sixteenth century was the land of the East Saxons; and several of them died in London. And in the nineteenth, choral singing, in "Associations", started in Cumberland and spread to Lancashire and the Isle of Man, and about the turn of the century reached Worcestershire, Somerset, and Hants. By 1910 Jersey, Aberdeen, and Cornwall. New Zealand, New South Wales and Canada had caught the infection. Soon after the war these associations were "federated" as "festivals", which means that for a small fee they became entitled to advice, help, publications, and so on, from a central council that does not in any way interfere with or control them. They have increased since then at an average rate of eight a year; this year (1932) is the Jubilee of one of the earliest, Stratford and East London.

These festivals are primarily local; they occasionally combine; there was a notable occasion at Liverpool a few years ago when seven choirs of fifty each combined in *Sweet Honeysucking Bees* under Geoffrey Shaw. But they compete a good deal, and that has been the making of them, as there is some indication that it was in the days of the madrigals. A certain amount of scorn has been poured on this competition; it is not music, they say; and there is a movement now in favour of not competing, which comes from some who do not like to be criticized in public. As to that, plenty of oars have survived the ordeal of being told from the bank, in the presence of their friends, that they had "round backs" or were "washing out" (*anglice*, shirking work); it seems as if the "non-competitors" might be well advised to grow a thicker skin. What do these little rubs matter to those who have the cause of music at heart? The problem of the judges is to be strict without being rude; and a body of experts has been gradually brought together for this purpose who do a deal of work, paid and sometimes unpaid, and who have the interests of the festival movement at heart. Another burning question is the notation: staff, or sol-fa? We are the only nation that clings to a letter notation, which is best for the voice; and it shows how deeply choral singing is in our bones. The solo voice is also encouraged, and that competition has resulted in the discovery of some good singers; there is a difficulty, however, in graduating the several ages properly.

One department of this organization was active a

few weeks ago at a delightful place called "The
Friends House" in Euston Road (where, by the by,
I saw over the doors the best lettering I have ever
seen anywhere). Dr. Armstrong, Mr. Ernest Read, and
Mr. Goldsborough were in three rooms teaching classes
of forty or fifty, chiefly schoolmistresses, how to conduct.
These schoolmistresses would go back to their villages
to face their choirs with a new confidence, born of knowing, now for the first time, what it is that a choir wants
from its conductor. Any member of the audience might
be called up—and I confess I cast a glance at the door
to see that a way of escape was clear—and be adroitly
urged into a position where he or she could become an
object lesson to the rest. By what the one or the other of
them forgot we saw how much there is to remember,
and how the thing that looks so simple in the concert
room is really an elaborate language, which is being
spoken all the time, mostly saying quite simple things,
but ready at any moment to say quite a difficult one.
Now the hand was too low; now the two hands were
tautologous; now the hand was moving and the stick
still; now the accompanist's help had not been enlisted;
now the place to breathe was not indicated, or slowing
and quickening were indicated that were not there.
The audience all had sticks and books, and conducted
the whole fifty imaginary choirs; all hoping secretly,
but fearfully, that they would presently be called upon
to provide sport.

It seems such a ridiculously easy thing to beat one,
two, three—for God Save the King, for instance—or
even to beat "one". I can do it with this toasting-fork
now.—There! ONE!—(to my own satisfaction); but

then there is no choir on the carpet, and no nervous feeling in my midriff that it all depends on me. The choir wants not only "one", but if it is to know when "two" comes (that is, how long to stay upon "one") it must know when the previous "three" came, so an indication of that must be given, but not so that someone away in a corner will think, by chance, that he is to sing to it. Again, no one can beat who does not keep his balance. He must stand straight up firmly. Women find this difficult; they sway, and crane. One of them told us she thought women had no poise, and the contest showed she meant no spine (or was it the two-and-a-half-inch heel?); of course, she would know best about that. But one *has* seen good women conductors. Of men, this nation possesses the best in the world. It is worth while to stand for ten minutes outside the Mansion House watching them. They have sticks, indeed, but they seldom take them out of their cases, which are usually hitched to a lamp-post. They wear white gauntlets instead, which are better seen than sticks in foggy weather. They stand immovable as the British Empire. One of them is responsible, and half a dozen others take their cue from him. If he turns his head, or shifts a foot, or lifts an eye-brow, or directs a glance, or shrugs a shoulder, or, as a last resource, raises a hand—that is as much as we ever see. You have only to be in some cathedral city, at a point where High Street and Fore Street meet, to see how much there is to learn about economy of gesture, and the lightning decision which alone makes it possible.

The business, then, of The British Federation of Musical Festival Competitions is to put heart into the

E

amateur, while The Incorporated Society of Musicians
sees to the professional. For the amateur's heart wants
taking care of. The weak point about him is that he goes
at a thing with a rush, and then drops it like a hot potato.
If each of these two hundred and twenty-seven festivals
(if I have counted right) would look upon itself as holding
a fort against Philistia, as most of them do, they would
have no doubt about the worth-whileness of it all.
Most of the really good work of this world, of England,
at any rate, is done by men who *give* their time and
money. (I was told once, but do not know if it was or
is true, that the Viceroy of India receives £30,000 and
spends £60,000.) The glory of the amateur is to give.
It is a glory that had a good deal to do with the making
of Greece and Rome.

CONDUCTORS

THE difference between one first-class conductor
and another with an orchestra of this eminence is
slight, though distinct. It consists of a minute drag on
the tempo to secure a vantage point later on (at the end
of "W.N.", before "Nimrod"), the exact calculation
of dynamics (at the change from minor to major in
Brahms's slow movement (4th symphony), or the crises
in Wagner). Of all such things two views are possible,
both equally justified. It is when at the end of an evening
there have been hundreds of such choices to make that
we begin to know which of these conductors is the man

for our money; though not every listener attends closely
enough to be able to form an opinion. Luckily, the
business of concert-going is not to form a comparative
estimate of the workmen, but to sink oneself deeper into
the work.

BOTTOM

THE audience estimates a conductor by what he
looks like more than by what he is. Like Bottom,
many a listener "goes but to see a noise that he has heard".

COMPOSERS

HAYDN

MUSIC has no history in the ordinary sense: it starts afresh with each composer whom the world has any reason to call great. Each of these makes a cameo, and the cameos can be strung together by anyone so minded; but no one can foresee what the next one will be.

The question before the world in 1760 was what was to happen about the wigs—about *den alten Zopf*. The full-bottomed—Bach and Handel—were gone; both were shelved in their native land, Handel remained only in conservative England; Bach's sons honoured their father, but turned round and went another way. The periwig remained, but who was to wear it, and how? About twelve years before, an Austrian, or rather a Croatian boy, had suggested the solution, by cutting off his schoolfellow's pigtail. He cut off simultaneously his own prospects in life, since he was promptly caned and dismissed the choir school, but his act hinted to an unwitting world that there would not be another "Hallelujah Chorus" or "Et Resurrexit", and that in the light-hearted, frothy Vienna the days of the mountainous fugue, complete with organ and kapellmeister, were numbered.

Franz Joseph Haydn (March 31, 1732—May 31, 1809) was the son of honest plebeian parents. They taught him industry (as leaked out in the noble chorus "O Fleiss" in *The Seasons*, his last work), method (and his belief in "form" is emphasized by the deliberate formlessness of his Chaos in *The Creation*), and religion (which may be read in the prayer and thanksgiving with which he approached and quitted every work he wrote, even a comic opera). Cast on the world at seventeen he had the usual struggles, which his biographers estimate in florins; we know a florin was two shillings, but as we do not know how much two shillings would buy there and then, we may pass all that and land him in Esterhaz at twenty-nine. Esterhaz was a marsh, which the Count Esterhazy who matters, Haydn's "my prince", Nicholas the magnificent, turned at a cost of 11,000,000 somethings into a second Versailles. Nicholas was strict and kind; Haydn was his lackey: a good thing for both, and for us too. For Nicholas, because Haydn's art kept him from treasons, stratagems, and spoils; for Haydn, because, though the chains clanked at times, the durance forced him, as he said, to be original; for us, because "a talent is bred in still waters, a character in the stream of the world".

Talent is commonly opposed in thought to genius, that up-welling quintessence of personality, but Goethe is not so opposing it here. He pictures talent as that slow, unceasing growth that neither thrives on opposition nor languishes from the lack of it, here a little and there a little, from the uncankered bud to the orbed

rondure; and character, as the windswept mountain
pine, its sap-rings all awry, but sound at heart. Haydn's
genius lay not in lightning decisions and divinations,
like Mozart's, but in the cumulative power of work
which distinguished him from his feckless, unequal
brother Michael. Like Rodney, who "had to" (beat
the French and de Grasse), his business in life was to
find out how to say worthily the light things the Viennese
wished to hear. He forwent the learned clichés of Graun,
and built his style on the solid knowledge of Fux and the
technical aptitude of C. P. E. Bach. And this style, as
pellucidly clear in the Weinzirl as in the Erdödy quartets,
was the lever by which he produced a revolution in the
art. There is nothing striking about it. A harmonic
invention or two has been pointed out, but we do not
feel that that was what he was aiming at. His running
counterpoints have been commended, but they are no
more than his ordinary parlance made a little more
fluid. As we go through a work we are made aware that
we are not in a battle but in a manœuvre; at the edge of
this wood or at that bridge-head there is a signpost,
"Out of bounds".

Its clarity is the thing: one thing at a time, and that
done thoroughly. He never lacks ideas, and he never
wastes them. His melodies are as much alike as first
cousins, but by the time he has given us the life history
of each they are quite distinct. He plays with them,
laughs at them, teases them, sobs over them a little perhaps, and then, for fear he should be getting too serious,
passes on to the next. The minuet is his darling. He started
life with two of them to a quartet, separated by an adagio;
the hundred and more he wrote are all different, and all

distinctive. As in the sonata movements for piano the distinction generally lies in the barring; there is no one who so convinces you, not even Mozart, that his odd bar-groups are really even. It was this facility which lay behind his mastery of form: form is, in fact, barring writ large. It is not because he wrote 84 quartets and 104 symphonies that he is the inventor of sonata form, but because, by everything he wrote, he established in music an articulated orderliness which was not there before.

The question before Haydn in 1760 was a different one. He was in love with a wigmaker's daughter. When he approached her father, J. P. Keller, he found she was destined for the veil; should he now, on the father's request, engage himself to the elder sister, Anna Maria, three years his senior? He married her on November 26. She bore him no children. She used his works for curl-papers and pastrycases, or occasionally badgered him into writing a motet, as an acceptable gift—from her, of course—to some Kapellmeister whom she had reasons for keeping well with. Perhaps because his wife—the "infernal creature", he called her—maltreated him, Haydn grew fond of Loigia Polzelli who, for her part, had grievances against her husband. Both Joseph and Loigia were waiting for two deaths. Polzelli died in 1790. Loigia, reflecting that Joseph was sixty-eight and she only forty (though she looked more), secured in writing a promise from him that he would marry none other, and that if he did not marry he would leave her a sub-stantial annuity. She gave him no promise in return, but on Anna Maria's death in 1800, immediately married someone else. His gay spirit and equable temper survived these buffets of fortune.

Haydn paid two visits to England (January 1, 1791, to end of June 1792, and February 4, 1794, to August 15, 1795) at the instigation of the concert agent, Saloman, whose enterprise enabled him just to intercept an intended visit to Naples. We seem to have worked him hard—he wrote 768 sheets of music here; to have paid him well enough to secure him an easy competence for his old age; and to have lionized him in our usual way, till at last he could accept no invitations except to titled houses. He wrote his best symphonies here, the twelve Salomans, and the *Creation* and *The Seasons* after his sojourn. Thus it was only at the end of his life—for his operas had had no real chance of success—that his melody was called upon to characterize. Quite broadly, though with exceptions, he succeeds with nature and fails with man. Few can miss in Gabriel's *With Verdure Clad* the joyous acceptance of the eternally unbelievable splendour of spring. And there is another piece of gentle eloquence in Luke's Cavatina, *Dem Druck erlieget die Natur*, the very voice of the swooning heat which precedes the thunderstorm. In a year or two more he wrote, with a pen dipped in the same impotence, that plaintive little phrase which he sent to friends who enquired after his health—"Gone is all my strength: old and weak am I"—and which is usually printed at the end of his quartets, his life work.

SIR CHARLES STANFORD

COMPOSER AND TEACHER

THE life of Sir Charles Stanford, by Mr. H. Plunket
Greene (Edward Arnold), was a difficult book to
write, and that may partly account for the delay; it is
(1935) eleven years since Stanford's death. He could
not have had a better biographer, hardly one so good.
The book is couched in terms of praise and, where
that is not possible, in the language of kindliness; but
the intention is none the less clear, that nothing is to be
concealed or extenuated. Sir Charles was wise and
witty. His wit was caustic, and that is not a crime but a
piece of unwisdom; it lost him friends, it lessened
opportunities, and it probably cost him the honour
he thought most worth having at his university. He never
understood Elgar, nor Elgar him: both were sensitive,
or—the obverse of the medal—touchy. Why not accept
the fact, as we accept a March wind, in which he died,
and forget it in April's sun and rain, in which he was
laid at the side of Purcell? Mr. Greene does, or else we
have misread his book. He confines himself to the facts
he knows, and sets these against things that have been
said, or are supposed to have been said, and there
leaves it.

    "In some ways it would have been better", we read,
"if he had been to a public school." But who can say?
Genius does not necessarily proclaim itself at thirteen,
and if it did, no one has as yet devised the proper training
for it. Genius is the combination of talent and character,

and Stanford indubitably had it. He saw straight to the
heart of a thing, saw the end and the means to it in one
glance. Mr. Greene finds this in his songs and the lightning skill of their writing. It is visible in all his works:
the one mark they all bear is the perfect security of
their technique, and he wrote in every style—symphony,
opera, concerto, quartet, church service. He knew, too,
how they should be played, who should do it, in what
order, on what occasion. He could conduct them so
as to get the best out of them without monopolizing time
at rehearsal that was the fair share of others. He had a
quite exceptional knowledge of composers, great and
less great, and a curious, almost disconcerting memory
for detail of their work.

In his own work one would be inclined to put first
the way he knew a tune when he heard one. It seems a
small thing to say, and yet everything depends at last
upon that power. There is so much that passes as music
which is mere essay-writing, and there were times, too,
when *he* did not rise above that—an organ sonata, a
pianoforte trio, perhaps; but for the most part he had
the gift of making his definite point and then sitting
down. This point he could throw into relief, yet not too
much relief, by the way he ground-baited for it, so to
say, and by the critical quickness with which he saw
how much ornament it would bear and what would
smother it. Not one of his works is grand, as a great
classic is grand; on the other hand, not one of them is
grandiose—he never mistakes the style and makes a
big thing say too little or a small thing too much.

That is what made him, by the confession of those
he taught, such a brilliant teacher. They have recorded

with pride and affection the way he used to tell them
that their composition came "from hell, H-E-double L,
my boy"; or "I'll tell ye what I'd do, I'd burn it"; or
(passing an undertaker's with the victim, after he had
had a whole afternoon to think over his lesson and wonder
what Stanford, who had said nothing, really thought of
his effort) "Take it in there, my boy". In the forty-one
years he was at the Royal College he had at least forty-
one pupils (probably twice that number) whose names
are known by their work to all musicians, and a dozen
of them to the world in general, as representative of
what is sometimes called the English Renaissance. One
of them he mentioned as, more than any, fulfilling the
accepted idea of a genius. This boy, a few years later,
dropped into some rooms in the Temple about 11 p.m.
He had walked from Gloucestershire the day before
and proposed to walk London the whole of that night:
all the great poets walked, he explained. He quoted
yards of Wordsworth and W. H. Davies; and I remember that the two diminished sevenths in *Ueber allen
Gipfeln ist Ruh* took us half an hour (he attacked both
and I defended the second on the analogy of the one in
Beethoven's funeral march). At half-past two he went
to sleep on the sofa, there being no spare room, and
before breakfast he was gone as he had come. When
others were writing their memories of Stanford, he
wrote this:—

> He was a stiff master, though a very kind man; difficult
> to please, and most glad to be pleased. England will bury
> many in the Abbey of Westminster much lesser than he.
> By him the German influence was defeated, and yet
> had good learnt of it. He was a born poet, but had to over-

come foreign form and influence. When England is less
foolish, she will think more of him. Had he been wiser,
he would have talked of Elizabethans at his lessons instead
of the lesser string quartets of Beethoven or the yet deader
things that industry and not conscience got out of the
German masters.

As for his work in Irish folksong arrangements, so
admirable, and his autobiographical books, stiff yet
charming, the first will last long; the second not long, but
will amuse worthily. Only the fools will deny that he
brought to them that Irish music, the best in the world,
then, of known folksongs.

That comes from the heart. And so does this, a shorter
one, from another pupil: "I went through Holland
Street on my way here and put my hand on the door
of No. 50 as I went by."

ELGAR'S MUSIC

ELGAR'S music owes the large place it holds in our
hearts to the fact that for us it bridges more than
any other the old and the new. That it is classical is
obvious; as Mr. G. B. Shaw said, "You may hear all
sorts of footsteps in it". And no one would deny that it
uses and exploits Wagner's harmonic apparatus, which
makes it modern for its day, roughly 1895–1915, or
more narrowly, the first decade of the century. It is true
that a new musical language, or languages, have been

in use since his day, but that he did not think it necessary
to invent one, entitles him the more to our respect.
Beyond merely exploiting Wagner's harmonic scheme
it is sometimes said that Elgar borrowed a good deal
from him. Perhaps it is such a moment as "O Jesu,
help" (*Gerontius*, p. 34, vocal score) in comparison
with the Wanderer's motive that is meant, the point
being in both cases a transformation of some kind.
But, first, the resemblance is too slight, and second,
poets do not really quote from each other; rather,
the instincts of both being true brings both, in so far
as there is a resemblance, to the same true result. The
fact is that he imitates no one, and that is how the
adjective "Elgarian" came into use; there is hardly any
composer who can tell you so certainly in two bars,
by the mere look of them, who he is.

As for his melodies, we each have our favourites:
some the "Graal"-like sound of the opening of the
A flat symphony, some the soaring two octaves of the
Introduction and Allegro or the rocket-like ascent and
descent immediately after the overture of *Gerontius*, others
the heaven-descending peace of the Alleluias in the
Apostles, or the theme of the slow movement of the
violin concerto which is its secular counterpart, or again
the flurry of the scherzo of the E flat. Such things can
at any rate be named in words; but what we are more
conscious of is all those nameless beauties that crop
up by the roadside, little gracious turns of phrase,
passing chuckles, pouts and pets, bits of bravado, of
slang, of devilry—and of "nobilmente". I used to have
an idea that he coined this word because he was too
modest to use the more usual "pomposo"; but it is in

the dictionary all right, and means "generously", and
that seems to be a word that an Englishman might use
without any of the pose that has frequently been hinted
at. Then the finger of scorn is pointed at *Land of hope
and glory*, and with some justification where it occurs
in the *Pomp and Circumstance* march, where there is the
same objection as to Polly Oliver in Holst's *Jupiter*.
But tunes are what their purpose makes them, and when
it is used for the same purpose as Sullivan's song about
Pay, pay, pay, it is better than a better one.

His texture is chromatic; and since that word is
grossly technical we must try to translate it. We all
know the feel of going from the minor to the major,
or the other way, because we speak of defeated politicians
as "singing in a minor key", and if anyone were to tell
us that the trade returns were bowling along "in C
major" we could give a good guess at his meaning.
Consider that change of feeling to be applicable all over
the music, so that every moment can become, by a turn
of the wrist, as it were, one of elation or depression,
and there you have chromaticism; and "texture" only
means that it applies to the chords as much as the tune.
But the elation and depression can also occur at the same
moment, and then you get chromatic dissonances
(chords that do not themselves make a satisfying close).
These chords then move the music onwards, like hand-
spikes that get a gun into position, and it is their business
to see that there is no dead point anywhere. It is a
speciality of Elgar's that he coins such phrases, and that
they become "motives", rallying points for the ear
which gets the sound of them by heart quite as well as
it does a bit of melody. They do not ticket anything,

in the way Wagner's sometimes do; it would be impossible to say that they "mean" anything in particular; but they have a sort of steadying influence among the wisps of cloudlike melody that fill the landscape.

In the orchestra of to-day everything can be played, but not everything will sound, and the composer's task is now more than ever to build his tuttis so that they do sound. Elgar's build is a model in that respect; the vertical combination is what the French call "well nourished". Contrast, for instance, the two tuttis in the fourth of the *Enigma*. The first is what an organist might call "half great with swell coupled" while the drums and trumpets only phrase; and the second is "all out", with trumpets and trombones nicely compact, but not so as to obscure the phrasing, nothing useless, a large sweep of sound but without noise; also, notice in the canon for two wind instruments that lies between, where the two melodies cross and might cancel each other, how two strings support them for a moment and keep them distinct. This is not in the least a show passage, and it is all far too easy and obvious for the wild men of to-day, who seem to think they are saying nothing unless they talk in whispers or roars. They are terribly ingenious, but few of them think instrumentally in the way Elgar does, so that the whole cake is thoroughly baked all through. He tried to understand the new point of view, but never succeeded. One cannot help thinking that he is right, and that the future of orchestration lies in a return to moderation and solidarity in some new form.

Elgar's music is to be enjoyed just because he enjoyed it so much himself. He liked good tunes, and the common idea of a tune is that it comes straight down from heaven. Of course, it does nothing of the kind; it is, as the Kingdom of Heaven is, like a mustard seed. The composer plans and shapes and orchestrates it till the meanest cannot miss it. But little minds do not think of great tunes. Elgar's mind was powerfully original, which is a way of saying that he did his own thinking, that he was directly and immediately himself in all he thought or did, that he was not merely "interested in" things, but was "in" them. He works with the old bricks and mortar of music with which Palestrina and Mozart had built, and makes of them something entrancing and quite new. Every one has thought of doubling the melody at the octave above or below, but how fresh it sounds at "Alleluia for evermore" (*Gerontius*, page 87)! Violins "divisi" is a common device; what mystery he adds at "this strange innermost abandonment" (page 22) by carrying it all through the strings! He revelled in these endless possibilities and had a child's pleasure in exhibiting his successes.

SIBELIUS

COCKTAILS, OR COLD WATER?

From this side and that we hear murmurs of the growing discontent with the new music, the new cacophony. We call it new, but it is a generation old, and that fact gives force to the murmurs. For the murmurers remembered that there was no excellent beauty that had not some strangeness in its proportions, that time is the only test of truth, that Bach was ignored for seventy years; and they waited. They are waiting still, but they find nothing that has improved on acquaintance. It all began as startling experiment; and when we hear Schönberg's *Pierrot* or Stravinsky's *Sacre* a second time it is still experiment, but has ceased to startle, which was all the merit it had. Their many imitators we have listened to as an intellectual duty, but not many of their pieces have we wished to hear a second time.

What seems to have brought the murmuring to a head is the way the B.B.C. has persistently, perhaps excessively, exploited this style. One understands their attitude. They are purveyors of news, and everything has a news value of some sort, but the value varies with the subject and the recipient. Purveyors of news are in much the same position as the sellers of books. The last music-hall song will sell for a couple of months furiously and then be dead; Gurney's *Power of Sound* was published in 1880, and the publisher is still disposing of copies. Thousands read the last murder; scores only have a place in their minds for the last discovered MS. of the New Testament. Broadly speaking, that has the greatest news value which implies the least previous knowledge. But the new cacophony implies much previous knowledge, for its method is almost wholly negative. It begins by saying "not romantic, not sentimental, not traditional", and it ends by being not human, not intelligible, not beautiful. A purely negative appeal like this can convey news only to the man who has a good deal of positive musical knowledge, who knows,

F

let us say, the sound of the principal symphonies of the
principal classical writers; and the man who after a
day of bulls and bears, or of fox and hounds, switches
on the wireless for himself, his wife and his cat, is not
often in that position. The B.B.C. is mistaken therefore
in supposing that cacophony is news to him.

There are a few, however, to whom this style is news,
and an article in the *Musical Times* tells us who they
are. They are the callow young to whom anything old
and great is irksome, who resent the tyranny of the
classics, who have not read history to any purpose
but simply say "We can't go on as we are", ignoramuses
who know little of music and do not want to learn more,
disgruntled people who are out of a job, failed composers who hope that extremism will pull some chestnuts
out of the fire, soppy people who see that the extremists
are in a minority and like to make martyrs of them.
(All this is rather meeting extreme by extreme.) The list
includes, finally, serious adherents, who cannot give a
reason for their faith. But this is asking too much.
What reason, after all, can we give for believing in such
a passage as the return of the subject in the slow movement of the *Unfinished*, or any other that we take to be
of consummate beauty? We may explain it in terms of
the German sixth or of the horn in E, but at bottom it
is just unaccountable genius, which decided that, then
and there, that thing was to be said and no other. We
cannot ask any of these composers to explain, but we
may, after a quarter of a century, make to them Plato's
request for a mode "that will imitate the tones and
accents of a brave man enduring danger or distress,
fighting with constancy against fortune; and also one

fitted for the work of peace, for prayer heard by the gods, for the successful persuasion or exhortation of men, and generally for the sober enjoyment of ease and prosperity"—a mode for courage and a mode for self-control. To this request they have not yet acceded.

But there *is* music which is written in one or other of these modes, and it is signed by various names, of which perhaps the chief are, in alphabetical order, Delius, Kodaly, Sibelius, Szymanowski and Vaughan Williams—each of us makes his own list. With these, and no doubt others, we hear, at their best moments, what comes, we feel, from a world remote from fear and desire. They do not "make" their music: it is "given" them to write. They do not know how they come to write it, they feel it must be so, something tells them it must. They do not invent new scales, like Busoni, nor a new intonation, like Bloch, nor patterns of notes, like Hauer; they do not mystify their audience by false analogies, like Scriabin, nor themselves by false magic, like Cyril Scott, nor do they suppose, with Strauss, that the purpose of music is to reproduce any sound that Nature or man can produce. Cosmopolitan, Hungarian, Finn, Pole, Englishman—they are of five nationalities and speak one universal, or European, language—music; each of them has achieved a style, and can, without fumbling or waste, say in it what he wants to.

Of one of these, J. T. Sibelius, Mr. Cecil Gray has just written a short life. He considers the country, the man, the works in general, and the symphonies in particular, in 200 pages. We know so little of any of these that almost anything he could tell us would be new. Perhaps we are, as he says, to blame for this, but there is not much time for specializing in most of our lives, nor enough money in most of our purses even if score reading could take the place of performance. But that is a fault we can mend, and have begun to mend, and Mr. Gray's book is a real help. He bases Sibelius's high position, first, on his large output—the last opus number is 116, and there are three dozen more works published without numbers—and second, on his symphonic mind. What is meant by this he shows by naming and discussing writers of symphonies who did not possess that mind, and his distinction, too long to give here, is sound. The book is temperately written: it contains not a single musical quotation (a sign of grace) and only one Swedish one, with which this article, as it began, shall now end. It is Sibelius to his German publisher—"Here abroad you mix cocktails of every colour, and now I come bringing plain cold water."

THOMAS TALLIS

EVERYONE has heard of Tallis's canon, set to Ken's *Evening Hymn*, and most people have sung the treble or the bass part of his Responses in utter ignorance that there was a tenor, ranging over three adjacent notes which they were intended, as a congregation, to sing. A few will have heard of his motet for eight five-part choirs, and a few more may have heard Vaughan

Williams's *Fantasia on a theme from Tallis*, or may know
No. 92 in the *English Hymnal*, which is that theme.
Some will connect him with Christopher Tye, of whose
age and general style he was, and with whom he con-
veniently alliterates; or with his friend, William Byrd,
of whose boy he was godfather, and with whom he was
the recipient of a "licence to print" music, of which
the first-fruits were his *Cantiones Sacrae* in 1575. There
or thereabouts ended the knowledge of one person,
at any rate, until the recent appearance of the sixth
volume of the *Tudor Church Music* (Oxford University
Press).

The name, Tallis, has a Norman-French sound
(like Talboys and tally-ho, from *taillis*), but is practically unknown otherwise. There is a faint indication
that he was a Leicestershire man. He died in 1585,
November 23, and his birth has to be guessed. In a
petition to the Queen for a lease of lands "in consideration of service," made and granted in 1577, he is described
as "verie aged". The editors think that may mean
that he was then seventy-two, and accordingly state
his birth as 1505 on the cover without a query. On the
other hand, Elizabethan mortality was much higher
than ours, and the "verie aged", though there is no
reason to think it exaggerated, was at least motived.
Moreover, his epitaph and a celebrated Latin poem
both speak with pride of his having lived under four
monarchs. If he had been born before Henry VIII's
accession (1509), the eulogists would hardly have failed
to know and to record the much more extraordinary
feat of having been alive in five reigns. Birth after 1509
would make him organist at Waltham Cross Abbey—

the first known date of his life—at an age at which White died.

To place him, we will take the year of Cranmer's letter to Henry VIII, 1544, which advised that the music of the Church should be of a "solemn note"; an expression of opinion which solidified three years later into the Royal Injunction that "no anthems were to be allowed but those of Our Lord, and they in English, set to a plain and distinct note, for every syllable one". It now became necessary either to adapt English words to the existing Latin masses (which was not easy) or to compose new ones. That year divides Tallis's (and Tye's) life almost equally. Byrd was two years old; White and Farrant were boys; Shepherd, Edwards, and Merbecke young men; Taverner (who died the next year) was in the prime of life; Fayrfax and Aston had been dead twenty years. Of these, Taverner, White, and Byrd have already appeared in this edition; Merbecke and Aston will do so; and the English church music of Tallis is still to come. Taverner was the last Englishman to write a mass on a secular tune, a thing which had been the recognized means of securing intelligible "form" for centuries past, and which the Council of Trent ('45–'62) definitely forbade. White illustrates the struggle to write music that would hang together without this prop; when we see the woodenly formal entries and the generally rigid logic of his eight-part *O praise God in His Holiness*, we with difficulty believe that the same man wrote the flexible melodies of his *Miserere* (the 51st Psalm, especially at "Behold, I was shapen in wickedness"). Tallis confronts the same problem. He can write the most hard-hearted piece of ingenuity as in *Miserere nostri*; there are seven voices (A–G, from high to low) arranged thus:—

A
B } independent strict canon at the unison.

C = F inverted and four times diminished (i.e. a quaver of C= a semibreve of F).

D = F inverted and once diminished.

E is a free part.

F is the TENOR (the theme).

G = F twice diminished.

Not much music, one imagines, would emerge from such austere conditions.

It might be supposed that a motet in forty real parts would be quite as austere. It is true that twenty of these parts announce the theme, "Spem in alium nunquam habui," in succession; but the theme changes its shape a good deal, and even if it could be heard after the first ten entries, it would not be monotonous. The second twenty change theirs, "praeter in te," still more. The whole forty are used for about a quarter of the time, partly by accumulation and partly in two sudden bursts. Dr. Mann's edition had, from exigencies of printing, to be on two facing pages, and was as difficult to read as a pianoforte duet by one pair of eyes. The whole forty are here on one page, and it is to be hoped we may now hear it again. It requires eight subconductors, and probably two voices to a part; and as voices differ much in penetrating quality it seems impossible to say which of many possible results we should hear. It probably takes six minutes, and ought to be sung twice with an interval.

But Tallis was by no means always writing enigmas. He has something of the impetus of White and the imagination of Byrd in the motets which the editors in their preface have held up to our admiration; and almost everywhere he has a sternness of his own. His melodies rarely ascend, and they lose expansiveness by not doing so; but they seem to float and "plane", and to find their way home as if they were live beings. He tries no harmonic flights; his staple is plain triads, and he is content merely to put occasionally the one you do not expect, at any rate in block harmony, which gives a feeling of bigness; and his "illegitimate" six-fours are apt to be impressive, as at "qui tollis peccata," in the four-part mass, which, however, depends on one MS. only. The editors do not think much of this mass; but is there not something rather touching in its gaunt unobtrusive texture, which we do not find in more florid treatment?

Puritan wrath was peculiarly hot against organs and choir books. Organs can be replaced, but the choir books, which lit bonfires, or were sent abroad to book-binders, cannot. A very small fraction of what there must have been at the dissolution of the monasteries is given, we will hope, a few more centuries of life in this fine edition. The volume is delightful to handle, though it is not for armchair reading—it weighs nearly 6lb., and is in other senses a thing to sit up to. The editors are laconic, and their silence is sometimes eloquent; the *Oxford History of Music* says that *O bone Jesu* is to be "probably unhesitatingly ascribed" (whatever that may mean) to Tallis; they have definitely hesitated to print it.

JOSEPH JOACHIM

L AST Sunday (28.6.31) was the centenary of Joseph Joachim, born at Kittsee, near Pressburg. This generation never really heard him, for his power over the bow began to fail at the end of the century. That power he took great pains to achieve, and violinists can tell us something about it and its effect upon the ears of those who heard it. But no man can explain the inexplicable—how it is that the human spirit can transmute itself into sound and speak direct to other human spirits. And it was this quality in his playing, this intimate voice whispering from mind to mind, that made him different from all players we have ever heard, because that mind held so much.

It held reverence. Wherever the soul of goodness lay in man or work he loved to discover it to others. He gave all their due; the great men first, but others in their order. He filled himself with the passionate immensity of Beethoven and the lyrical steadfastness of Bach, and so became aware before anyone else of the security of purpose that lay deep in the nature of Brahms. Many talk of the three B.'s: he lived them, by making them vital. He showed us by his method of approach how far we often are from being fit company for the great. His answer to the waywardness that picks and chooses was to show how much it had missed in what it turned away from. The modesty that endeared him so especially to our nation, that spoke in so many little actions and quaint sayings, was the outward sign of this inward reverence.

It reacted also on others. He brought together and, what is much more, kept in being a famous quartet. A quartet is not a mere combination, as it is often called. It is a living whole. A little fault of temper will wreck that, as surely as it will send a "coxswain-less" four to the bottom of the river. It is the captain who keeps the temper of his crew; and he does it by remembering always that the whole is greater than the part. Joachim set the example of self-effacement. He played his part *sub specie aeternitatis*—as it would look in the eyes of eternity. That sounds rather tremendous; but he also could ripple over into fun, irresponsible, sly, grey-eyed as Athene's, or innocent as Lewis Carroll's. Over these lightning conductors of fun and modesty the levin of naughtiness passed harmless to the ground.

The quartet was in existence from 1869 to 1907, the year of his death. We may take a bird's-eye view of it:—

Age.		
Leader's.	Average.	
38	40	Began, with Schiever, de Ahna, and Müller.
41	44	Rappoldi (viola) came, and de Ahna moved to second violin.
46	45	Wirth (viola) replaced Rappoldi, who went to Dresden.
48	41	Hausmann (violoncello) replaced Müller, whose interest was in an orchestra.
61	45	Kruse (violin) replaced de Ahna, who had died.
66	50	Halir (violin) replaced Kruse, who came to England.
76	60	Ended, with Halir, Wirth, and Hausmann.

The leader spent exactly half of his life in the quartet:

so did Hausmann; and Wirth and de Ahna nearly the same proportion of their lives. Joachim was, during the whole time, head of the Hochschule at Berlin, which he raised to a high position; and all of these men came at one time or another to teach there under him. Schiever left the quartet to come to Liverpool, where he led the Richter orchestra; de Ahna, an Austrian, of gentle bearing and with a refined style, found, after eight gruelling years in the army, a home in the Royal orchestra at Berlin. Wilhelm Müller came of a famous family. His father, Karl, and three uncles formed a string quartet, in the first third of the century, which gave the first great lift to chamber music: and in the second third, he and his three brothers started another, but turned before long to orchestral music. Hausmann was the pupil of Wilhelm and of his uncle Theodor. Wirth made a name as a violinist, and died at a great age. Kruse settled in London, where he revived the Saturday Popular Concerts, and alone of them all is still living.

Joachim's constant visits to this country—bringing latterly his quartet with him every year—taught us a great deal. He speaks warmly in his letters to Brahms of the "good musicians" and what they think—Parry, Grove, Stanford, and others. He liked to come, as Brahms disliked the idea of coming—though probably there was no more behind this than the terrible thought of getting into "Frack" (boiled shirt) and facing Mrs. Leo Hunter. And we liked having him here for his pure geniality as well as for his music. For he was simply pleased with simple things, a common mark of greatness, and was always good company because he could put people at their ease. What he taught us was to hear with fresh ears. He could take things like Beethoven's concerto, that we thought we all knew, and make it sound as if for the first time; or things like Ernst's Fantasia on Rossini's *Otello*, that we thought common, and make it sound uncommon—so true it is that beauty is in the eye of the beholder and in the ear of the listener.

There has seldom, more probably never, been a composer who could not play an instrument, and rarely an executant who had not also turned at some time to composition. Among those executants Joachim stands high, and his Hungarian concerto is valued for its own sake as well as for his. Moreover, unlike some other executants, he was drawn to composition by no desire of exploiting his instrument, but by the prospect it offered of uttering by a new means the music that was in him. In that matter one could have wished him, perhaps, a less learned and more practical teacher than Moritz Hauptmann. But the fact that he tried seriously to compose had as its great and lasting result the help that he was able to give Brahms. Their friendship was lifelong; neither did anything without consulting the other, or at least hoping that it would win his approval. They fell out once or twice, as the best friends will, and perhaps should, for the joy of coming together again. When a man is quite at the top of his profession he is very much alone, and a real friend is more to him than to most. In this friendship each shared the hopes and soothed the fears of the other, and the work of both was the better for it. That it was so is one of the great facts of musical history on which memory delights to dwell.

SENSIBILITY AND VULGARITY

A<small>N</small> esteemed acquaintance told the writer he was pained at reading somewhere that Tchaikovsky's music was vulgar, because as a matter of fact he *liked* Tchaikovsky's music. He was, further, good enough to say that the *Observer* ought to have an article on Vulgarity in Music, and that it was that sort of thing that he paid twopence for. The writer, meanwhile, has "as a matter of fact" for some years past thought of that very topic as a subject, but rejected it as too vague and too difficult to say anything on that would be of use.

There is one sense of the word vulgar we must get out of the way first. When H. M. Butler was, we are told, solaced in his sickness by Pickwick—"How I do love him, and how fearfully vulgar almost every page of him is!"—he meant, no doubt, the fearful joy with which a man tastes humour some shades below his own delicate sense of it. But he meant also that humanity which spoke once to Cecil Sharp with the tongue of an Appalachian mother-of-a-family—"We are sorry you are going, we like you both; you are so nice and common." That is the sense in which the good music-hall tunes are vulgar: they breathe a spirit of all-friends-here and no-exclusiveness. Sullivan was vulgar in that sense. He might have made play in *Mikado* with the local colour that Puccini afterwards put into *Madame Butterfly*, or have dropped in *Patience* into the sham sentiment of Offenbach's *Barcarolle*. But he never did; and he never wrote a note that everybody could not endorse.

The music-hall tune is vulgar in the sense of "low"

when it takes not the average but the least common multiple of the intelligence of its patrons. This results in its confining itself to obvious intervals (which point one way and can therefore disappoint, as is the intention, by going another) and monotonous rhythms (where nobody can possibly "get out", and therefore everybody is thoroughly "in it"). The notes themselves are as good as gold, and no wonder, since they frequently come, thinly disguised, from the classics; most of the naughtiness they contain is in the grace-notes—slick smartness or languorous glides—and in the accompanying gestures, which succeeded in shocking the past century as much as they fail to satisfy the present.

That the vulgar tune has its origin in the classical language is enlightening: the tunefulness, as we see, is taken and the art left. Conversely, many humble people can write original tunes that, with a little shaping, would make hymn-tunes, folksong, or music-hall song as the case might be, but have not the faintest idea how to go on, or what to do with them except to repeat. It is the eternal difference between those who have an idea and those who can, as R. L. S. says, "rub two ideas together while waiting for the train"—the difference between fancy and imagination. Upstanding music, music which can't help "going on", begins at imagination and stands or falls by the wealth or the lack of that. Since what we judge in a musical work is the quality of the imagination, and since that covers the whole work (for it would be impossible that part should be imagined and part not) the judgment is of the whole, not of a part. It is also equally open to all, and not the monopoly of a few pundits.

Examining then each work as a whole, we find the maximum of sensibility in Mozart. He imagines out. He sees the end in the beginning. He has such an eye for country that he never comes across the oxers and raspers that others boast of having negotiated. He keeps one key longer than any contemporary because he finds so much to say in it, and the change of key, when it comes, means so much the more. "Music", he says of the song where Osmin breathes threatenings and slaughters, "must never, even in the most terrific situation, give pain to the ear"; and accordingly the key he chooses is no farther off than first-cousin once removed to the one he leaves. Again, in the final quintet, when the stanza has been sung four times already and Osmin, whose turn it is, ought to know it by now, the only revenge Mozart takes is to make him barge in before his time and then lose his key (like John in *Hugh the Drover*). Beethoven's Pizarro loses something in comparison with this by its violence, and Wagner's Beckmesser by its cheap caricature. Then again Mozart never makes a noise. His climax, when it comes (and never before its time), is one not of superimposed volume but of inherent complexity; just as George Eliot's Romola dies not by a catastrophe but because he had himself made life too complicated to live out.

When people call Tchaikovsky (or, in their various ways, Offenbach, Gounod, Meyerbeer, or Elgar) vulgar, they do not mean, as is sometimes thought, to impute some moral, social, or intellectual stigma. They are clutching at a word to describe a disapproval they have not yet analysed, but which turns out to be a dislike of the tendency to overpaint or to under-imagine. Composers overpaint when they depart from solidarity and run a single aspect of the matter to death, it may be a particular harmony, a special metrical element, a favourite figure or modulation. Tchaikovsky overdid his climax (in the "1812"), climaxed in a fidgety way and too often (in the Fourth Symphony, finale), sentimentalized (finale of the Sixth), and misused the pianoforte as a percussion instrument (concerto) in which he antedated an evil of to-day. He under-imagined when he made most of his tunes eight or sixteen bars long, let his basses saw away regardless on tonic dominant, chopped his theme into scrappy lengths instead of laying it on the plate in neat slices, or gingered up his diatonic with his inevitable appoggiaturas. All the same, he wrote much sound music (*Nutcracker Suite*), with a fine sweep (concerto, first movement) and strong rhythm (scherzo of sixth), and many dainty album pieces (for pianoforte), and he had, like Schubert, a knack of true counterpoint which hits the mark without pretence. For these reasons the writer, too, "likes" Tchaikovsky.

YOUNG BRITISH COMPOSERS

IT would be idle to deny that the Broadcasting Corporation has now taken a decisive part in musical politics: few things are now the same as they found them when their activities began. There is nothing derogatory to their prestige in the request that they should put the position of their musical statesmen—if that is the right word—beyond cavil by taking responsible expert advice on a matter which is largely technical. By force of circumstances they have stepped into the position of "editor" of all the music of this country, and an editor has to take advice on technical matters. The questions on which advice is needed are such as these—What proportion should be struck as between the old and the new? What proportion as between native and foreign? What particular works in the two categories (new native and new foreign) should be heard now? These questions and others that may arise out of them can hardly be settled out of hand; they are matter for consideration and debate. The plea here is that the best musical opinion should be called in for that purpose. We have seen a mistake already made by neglecting to do this, when the opera subsidy was given by the Government of the day without asking for the views of musicians whom that point concerned. Here is another such point.

It is commonly understood (and if not the case, it can be contradicted) that the programmes of the B.B.C. are in the hands of a committee of half-a-dozen, and that among these the conductor has no deciding voice; in fact, he told us in one of three recent lectures at the Royal Institution that the final selection depended on diverse considerations which did not come within his purview. If his musical judgment is not decisive, we not unnaturally wish to know whose musical judgment is, that we may judge for ourselves of his or their qualifications. A little time ago, when the question was asked who settled the programmes, someone in the B.B.C. replied (in an analytical concert programme) by giving certain prominent names as those of their musical

G

advisers. But what they were asked was not who advised, but who settled the programmes; and these gentlemen have not as yet told us whether the programmes are in fact submitted to them, or whether their advice, if given, is taken. The actual names commanded respect, but there was no indication that they accepted responsibility as a body; so that we are still in the position of not knowing who does accept it. A more satisfactory way would be to have a committee, nominated by the Corporation's own musical advisers, proposed to, and ratified by, a public meeting of those who represent the musical institutions of London and the provinces; to pay them for their work (not a light one) and to publish their names.

The crux of this matter of programme selection is the proportion of native to foreign. A year or so ago a similar question was raised in an acute form by the Incorporated Society of Musicians. Their advocacy of native executants met with opposition because they did not put it on the right grounds. At worst they said "Buy British", which might be interpreted as a commercialism which has nothing to do with art; and at best, "native is as good as foreign", which may be true or not, but depends on the particular instance. In the case of the young composers there is a truer ground. We have to consider what is best for the country. What is best for any country is an art which is in every possible way in accord with its manner of thinking, and what is worst is for it to go a-whoring after strange gods. English music "tastes" better to Englishmen, as Wiltshire bacon than Danish. We seldom notice this till we have to do without it. Why else, when we walk along the Dover platform and see after a long absence, young Britons in flannels, do we keep muttering, "I'm sure I know that man", or if we don't know him, feel we should like to? What else is meant by "Sie küsste mich auf Deutsch, und sprach auf Deutsch, Man glaube kaum wie süss es klang", or by Debussy's "musicien français"? Englishmen's music—Wilbye, Purcell, Wesley, Parry—has solid, undemonstrative qualities, and is apt to be better than its word. I have before me a list of young men, who would benefit by a little encouragement, which I could show to anyone who could take action.

What action is required, and who should take it? It is obvious that such of these composers' works should be performed as the best musical opinion should recommend. Secondly, that, if they deserved it, provision should be made for a second or third performance. Thirdly, from the best of them, a work ought to be commissioned for a special occasion. That used to be done by individuals and corporations: now that the Broadcasting Corporation has drawn all the threads of concert-giving into its hands and has left other agencies to a precarious existence, all three tasks fall morally to them. They have not yet realized that duty, for Dr. Boult, in the current number of the *Royal College of Music Magazine*, has stated their policy. He says that the B.B.C. "cannot give time to young composers to try experiments" (in orchestration), for which the Patron's Fund supplies the proper opportunity; and that it "cannot help young performers to get their experience". He adds that there is a "long waiting list of performers and composers", and that this has now been drastically curtailed.

It is not experiments in orchestration that are wanted, but occasions to write at all. The Patron's Fund performs compositions about three times a year, and entries are dropping off. And why is that, except that no one holds out a helping hand? Wireless could not in any case give experience in performance—at least, only in microphone performance; but, having removed, to some extent, the opportunities executants had of getting engagements, it ought, to some extent, to provide others. And as for the waiting list, does Hindemith take his place in the queue, or has he sent his messenger-boy to keep it for him; or may we hope that he has by now received one of those circulars that were sent to thousands of applicants? The public at large are well content with what wireless has done for them. The majority of those who care for music will wish for the classics, which were chiefly written by Germans. Nothing said here will touch either of those interests. The two pleas are: (1) that in such time as can be allotted to modern music a definite and deliberate policy should be maintained of fostering young British talent in composition, and (2) that the best musical judgment of the country should be exercised upon that policy. No favour is being asked for, it is a matter of justice.

THE SCOPE OF CRITICISM

An entirely heartening lecture was delivered last week (April 1931) by Mr. W. R. Anderson, on Elgar's music. The *Enigma Variations* and the *A Flat*

Symphony were expounded piecemeal on the gramophone, and then played through without a break—variation by variation and movement by movement. As the one takes twenty-five minutes or so, and the other forty, this meant that comment had to be quick, precise, and pointed: and it was. Moreover, the luxury of having the performance managed by an expert with a minimum of break—a second or two—and that only occasionally, when the disc or the side of it had to be changed, was a real boon. I may honestly say that it is the first time I have really enjoyed the gramophone.

But, then, I was listening to it critically, with the score, and imagining the things that it sometimes only adumbrated. There certainly are a good many things that do not come out, or come off; but everyone knows that, and makes allowances. What is really valuable is the picture as a whole, and the fact that any special bit can be turned on again and again for study. Also the conductor's readings (in this case the composer's) are all there, and the tempi, and even the best score-readers (of whom I am not one) like to be reminded, by the sound, of the general proportions, and of details that the eye easily misses. As for people who listen for three-quarters of an hour on end without a score, one can only say that they must be exceptional enthusiasts.

Mr. Anderson is an enthusiast, too—a sane one, but determined. He speaks of things as he hopes they are, and as he wishes them to be; he does not weigh pros and cons and strike a balance—at least, not in a lecture. Most people will agree with him in that. The world wishes to hear pleasant things: unpleasant things provoke thought and it does not, as a rule, wish to think.

The lecturer also spoke, however, of adverse criticism as "denigration". We ought to discuss this. Since everyone does not know what has happened, we must narrate. Professor Dent wrote last year a short perspicuous account of English music for the chief German musical history. His article (550 lines) mentions about forty composers: it gives 32 lines to Parry and Stanford together, 34 to Parry and 42 to Stanford alone, 21 to Sullivan, 16 to Elgar, 35 to Vaughan Williams, 19 to Holst, 24 to Delius; most of the rest have from one to six lines (the length is affected by the fact of their writing or not writing opera). The bulk of the article is taken up with a discussion of tendencies and principles. As far as it counts at all, this variety of length is a rough estimate not of the merits of individuals but of their influence as members of a school of music upon their century. The gist of what is said about Elgar's music is as follows:—

Elgar began music later in life (than Parry and Stanford) and astonished people by the brilliancy of his orchestration and the warmth of his feeling. He was a violin player, and studied Liszt—an abomination to the academics. He was a Catholic and self-taught, and he had little opportunity of the literary training of Parry and Stanford. For English ears his music is over-emotional and not without a tang of vulgarity. His orchestral works are written with vivid colour, in a showy style and with an affected gallantry of expression. The finest of them is *Falstaff*, which is weakened, however, by too close dependence upon the programme; all the same, it is a work of great power and originality. His chamber-music is dry and academic.

On this followed a manifesto addressed to the readers of German newspapers, signed by a dozen professional musicians and half-a-dozen others; it would have been stronger if the signature had contained more than two of the names mentioned in the article. This protests that the article in question is "unjust and inadequate", and challenges the statements that "for English ears the music is much too emotional and not free from vulgarity", that all the orchestral works are "lively in colour, but pompous in style and of a too deliberate nobility of expression", and that the chamber-music is "dry and academic". A note appended to his signature by Mr. Shaw asserts that Elgar is to England what Beethoven is to Germany, equates the "vulgarity" to that of *See the Conquering Hero* or the finale of the Fifth Symphony and claims for the basis of *The Apostles* and *The Kingdom*, a "literary training undreamt of by Parry and Stanford." (The text is to be seen in the current number of the *Musical Times*.) On this question of vulgarity there may be more to be said at some other time.

A manifesto is a doubtful procedure: German readers may, incidentally, be reminded of one that Brahms lived to regret, like Luther, who "called the Epistle of James an epistle of straw, and was sorry for it afterwards". Also, if it is difficult for a single man to be sure what he means by a given form of words, it is impossible for a body of men. From the correspondence which ensued, the gravamen of the protest seemed to lie in Professor Dent's claim by the phrase, "for English ears", to speak for the English public. But does he make any such claim? Take three other sentences of his which occur in the article.

The English nature regards vocal music as a more natural means of expression than instrumental.

Henley's *Last Post* is too consciously imperialistic for English feeling of to-day.

Delius's treatment of the words in *Sea-drift*, *Mass of Life*, and *Requiem*, is, for English ears, weak and spiritless.

Can we suppose that anyone who might have written these was speaking really of his own nature or feelings or ears, but intending to speak for the public? Dent is saying, from a closer investigation than many have made of our musical history, what he believes the Englishness of us all desires He may be right or wrong about that; he is not arrogant.

Criticism must be thought-provoking; it may be imaginative; it should be true; it can never be final. Nobody will object to its being the first two of these, or demand that it should be the last. The question is whether it is true. As long as minds are individual, that is, compact of specific qualities, the truth they can speak must be relative, not absolute—your truth is not mine, and so on. Truth of judgment cannot be proved or disproved, like truth of fact. It can sometimes be supported or discredited by argument, but mostly not, being intuitive. To controvert it is at once to appeal to the person behind it: which of the two is to be believed? In a choice of action in difficult circumstances we often ask a friend's advice with neither intent nor obligation to follow it: we want it merely to help us to think. It is the same with a critical judgment. In uttering the best truth it knows, it helps us to think; its sole basis is the *ipse dixit* of a person; we may read it or ignore it. If it does not give us the help we wanted we shall not go to that friend again. Now that he has been publicly trounced and roundly rebuked for what is deemed the error of his ways, it is likely that many will steal silently back to this particular friend for his counsel on difficult matters.

INSPIRATION

WHATEVER man knows, exists already; what he imagines, he creates. The composer imagines. He may imagine anything, of course; though in practice there are two pretty stringent limitations to this. The executant imagines, and his scope is narrower; though until he exercises his imagination, the composer's work cannot be said truly to exist. Audiences imagine to varying degrees: from the audience which attends Donald Tovey's recital, to which no one would go who did not put music first, down to that which eats its supper to a band, which no one would do who did not put music last, there is one long hierarchy of imagination and of creation; for in proportion as the listener does not imagine, the music does not exist for him. To imagine is not so easy as to think, and that is hard enough— at least, people will often accept and adopt printed thought, and will then sometimes revile the Press for their tyranny in thinking it. Also, some will think a thing out, but few will imagine it out.

In defence of this sweeping statement I would cite the case of *The Rosary*, which has been translated into

eight languages (including Esperanto), arranged for
fifty different combinations, vocal and instrumental, and
sold since 1898 to more than a million purchasers.
If you look at that song—constructed, in a general way,
on the unobtrusive lines of the hymn tune, *Peace,
Perfect Peace*—you will find that Mr. Nevin has imagined
one thing only. He makes the voice fall, while the
accompaniment rises, by semitones:

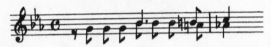

This occurs four times, veiled, the third and fourth
times, by an extensive figure in the accompaniment
(I quote from memory):

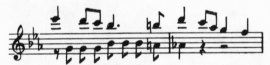

and this figure, like a similar one in *The Honeysuckle
and the Bee*, is half-remembered from *Lohengrin* and
Samson and Delilah. This develops into

and an enthusiastic singer has commended these phrases
for the apt way in which they illustrate the beads of the
rosary, ten red punctuated by one black one. There,
with the necessary cadences, you have the whole melody.
The words, by R. C. Rogers, discreetly combine an
allusion to the one Divine name (which enabled the song
to be sung on Sunday—not unimportant as a monetary

consideration, at the end of the last century) with a
tacit reference to any feminine appellation which a million
devout lovers and singers might severally care to supply.
The euphonious title, which offers to the purchaser,
according to his antecedents, an everyday fact, a metaphor, or a mystery, or even suggests flowers, is a stroke
of genius. Upon this song has been expended as much
loving care as on a Gillette razor, and as much imagination as belongs to a successful soap. Mr. Nevin, with
the experience of forty-seven songs behind him, could
doubtless have put more imagination into this one;
but he dared not, because he knew his prospective
audience would not be able to go with him all the way.

BEETHOVEN—CENTENARY LITERATURE

Mr. SONNECK's book, about the "immortally beloved",
may be strongly recommended to all unmusical
people. Recommended, because the evidence is most
carefully gathered and sifted; and unmusical people,
because the subject throws the minimum of light upon
Beethoven's character and none on his music. In point
of interest it ranges between a detective story and
"demon" patience—rather nearer the latter. There is
no room here to do more than state the problem
for those who do not happen to know it. Beethoven
wrote an authentic, passionate, and sincere love-letter
to someone who lived at K., from somewhere, on
Monday, July 6th (with a postscript on Tuesday,

July 7th), in some year. Assuming Beethoven to have
been right, that the Monday on which he wrote was, in
fact, the 6th July—and there are a score of instances of
his misdating in the 1,500 letters we have, most of which
are dated—the years when July 7th fell on a Monday
are 1801, 1807, 1812. Of these 1812 has been shown
to be almost certain. The letter is thought to have been
written from Teplitz, and K. to be Karlsbad. As many
ladies are candidates for the honour of being the "immortally beloved" as towns for the honour of being
Homer's birthplace. Mr. Sonneck gives on his last page
the conditions to which the successful candidate must
conform. Three of the seven candidates remain possible,
but he refrains from adding what is only too obvious,
that if we knew for certain which of them it was we
should be no wiser, for they are mere names.

ON ALTERING THE MUSIC

IT is common to hear a performer praised for "letting
the music speak for itself", as if virtue could be a
negative thing (in spite of Aristotle). There is no "letting"
about it: he *made* it speak for itself by doing certain
positive things. Busoni, for instance, did a good many
positive things. He allowed, his biographer reminds
us, "no undertones, no half-statements, no evasions . . .
he played the Trio of Chopin's *Funeral March* like a
cornet solo because 'if you honestly believe the melody
is beautiful you must sing it with all the fullness of your

voice'. . . . 'Never look back', he said, and played
nothing that he could not regard and interpret as pro-
phetic of the future." Those interpretations are gone,
though some transcriptions remain; and when we hear
these transcriptions, everything is there—but Busoni.

> O, ye mistook; ye should have snatched his wand,
> And bound him fast; without his rod reversed,
> And backward mutters of dissevering power,
> We cannot free the lady that sits here
> In stony fetters fix'd.

And there is Chaliapin. Who would ask that he should
"let" the music do anything but what he makes it do?
He, too, makes composers say what they never thought
of saying, but might well wish they had. In a hundred
little ways he alters what "it puts"; very wrong of him,
and yet we say, how right! And behind Chaliapin there
are the singers of the past who, under the name of
"graces", did with the composer's work and with his
consent, what they liked, and who, when they did it with
taste, made themselves famous.

CHOPIN, AGAIN

CHOPIN was an aristocrat at heart. He loved the
amenities: polite speech, genuine courtesy, careful
dress, flowers, educated talk. His biographer lets drop
somewhere the word "snobbish", but one does not quite
see why. Snobbery is pharisaical. It plumes itself on

something that came by the accident of birth, education, money, and so forth. There is nothing snobbish in having the perception to see that good things *are* good, and therefore preferring them to mediocre things that satisfy less percipient minds.

The moral of this book is rather a sad one for us: we see in it one of the reasons why the English are not thought, except by themselves, to be musical. Chopin disliked the English, and Mr. Murdoch hints, with some truth, at prejudice. He came among us and was flabbergasted at the indifference to adequate rehearsal and at the attitude of the audience; he noted it also as a curious thing that we reserve the word "art" for pictures, and call music a "profession". We might find, and we do find, much to say on the other side; but here is one whom no one doubts to have been a consummate artist, saying that we do not understand what music really is. From another side, also, the same truth is borne in upon us. Could such a man as Chopin have lived and exercised his art in England; in fact, to put it quite bluntly, do we not kill off early all our potential composers by the Procrustes-bed of our citizenship? It is not—Could we do more for this or that promising lad? but—Do we or can we allow any promising lad who may turn up to be unbearable like Beethoven, conceited like Wagner, feckless like Schubert, or constitutionally miserable like Chopin? And if we cannot, can we expect to have any out-and-out composers? Have we ever reached the thought that music may be an end in itself—something worth living for, and, if need be, dying for?—that is one question that Chopin's life puts to us.

HANDEL

ANOTHER test of a biography is, how far it puts us *there*, in the man's life as he lived it, among his contemporaries as they influenced him. That is what Professor Dent's life of Handel in the "Great Lives" series (Duckworth) does conspicuously well. It is the shortest of stories about a long and full life. The original account of Handel, written the year after his death, is untrustworthy; the letters, which do not tell us much, amount in all to a score; beyond those two sources there is what Burney and Hawkins happened to remember sixteen years later. In such circumstances what is to be done? Mr. Dent shows us how much can still be made clear as to what it meant to be alive in the eighteenth century in Germany, Italy and England, and to write music and make a living; what others were writing and thinking; what helps and hindrances were met with; what was printed, and how; what fashions came and went; what powers rose and subsided. His book makes us feel as if we were living in Handel's time, because that is where he lives himself in thought, at any rate for the moment.

In this dearth of actual knowledge myths of all sorts have had birth and flourished, and have sometimes been pointed in a particular sense to suit this or that biographer. A short way is taken with them here. They are rationalized, perhaps, as with the story of the child Handel smuggling a clavichord into the garret, a rather heavy thing for a boy of seven to lift; it is quietly hinted that the father did not forbid, only was irritated (as sane people are with street music), and the mother arranged it all for the peace of the household. Or they are just exploded.

The "Harmonious Blacksmith" was a nickname of a music-seller who had been a blacksmith's apprentice at Bath in 1820, given him because he was always singing the air from *Suite de Pièces pour Clavecin.* The name was somehow transferred from singer to song. A letter to *The Times* in 1835 stated that Handel composed the air out of the musical notes he heard from an anvil at Edgware, to suit which a blacksmith at Edgware was invented, and his anvil not long afterwards sold by auction. One ventures to lift this incident bodily from Mr. Dent's book, because the more people who understand that suites are not made from anvils (nor sonatas from moonshine) the better.

AUTOGRAPHS

HANDEL'S paper was the best of his age with ten staves to the page ready printed for him; the slope of the quaver triplets and the quick dash across their tails show the pace at which he wrote; he seldom changes his mind, but where he does he is apt to make a fearful mess of the page (or pages). Bach must have found paper scarce from the way he economizes it. He rules twenty staves to the page with a five-line roller (you see it wobbling between the alto stave and voice) which sometimes clogs, and then he squeezes in a twenty-

first stave to make up; there is no haste, he draws
straight bar-lines and gets the notes properly under
each other; when he finds himself a stave or two
short he uses lute tablature (which requires none);
when he changes his mind he corrects clearly or else
re-writes. Both upset the inkpot occasionally and get
hairs in their pen, and no doubt they characterized
the incident much as the violent and the placid man
would to-day.

BIOGRAPHY

A BIOGRAPHY should put us in possession of the man's
tone of mind, and it should contain everything that
may conceivably do this and nothing that may not.
Thus it may conceivably be important what he had for
breakfast, and when he bought a new waistcoat, and
even what τὸ θῆλυ thought of it, and quite unimportant
whether he had three wives or one, and this disease or
that. What matters is what he made of it all. For wives
and waistcoats count—at least "where heroes are"—
only to the extent to which they test him and bring out
his character; and his comment, if there was one, on an
underboiled egg at breakfast—a time when no man is
at his best—may just possibly illuminate that.

Musical biographers seem, however, not to have
sufficiently digested this platitude. They tell us far too
much of what other people thought of their hero and
not enough of what he thought of them. They dish up
old concert notices, long decently buried in the news-

H

paper room of the British Museum, in order to convince us that his voice, which we have never heard, was exceptional—as if all our special friends were not exceptional in that respect—or his method impeccable— as if it were ever worth while to insult a man's feelings by hinting at imperfection which it is now too late for him to cure. Or they weigh his voice, or more often hers, against dollars received, as the souls are weighed by the archangel over the door of St. Michael's, Cornhill.

BYPATHS

THE NATIONAL ANTHEM

(I) THE WORDS

WITH a song like our National Anthem, where words and tune are absolutely inseparable, a musical writer may reasonably, for once, discuss the words only. The question is raised by a letter written to the Dean of Worcester, and recently printed in *The Times*. The writer is pained by the use in church of the second stanza, and asks for measures to be taken to substitute something else at future meetings of the Three Choirs.

As to the authorship of the words, as the writer says, nobody knows and nobody cares. We may care, however, if we think of altering them again, what they originally were, how they were first altered, and when. The form in which they first appeared in print is two-fold; there was a Latin version provided for the birthday of the Princess of Wales, which was on November 28, 1743 (old style), and an English one in the first volume of *Thesaurus Musicus* published by J. Simpson soon after May 3, 1744. The English version appears with the tune

we know, but in a slightly different form; and it is reasonable to suppose, though there is no proof, that the Latin
was sung to the same tune. The original English words
and tune are given correctly in Grove; only the
date is wrong.

The *Birthday Book* in which W. H. Cummings
found the Latin words is now in the Leeds Library.
They appear also in Julian, but not in Grove. We had
better look at them.

> O Deus Optime!
> Salvum nunc facito
>   Regem nostrum;
> Sit laeta victoria,
> Comes et gloria,
> Salvum jam facito
>   Tu Dominum.

> Exsurgat Dominus;
> Rebelles dissipet,
>   Et reprimat:
> Dolos confundito;
> Fraudes depellito;
> In Te sit sita spes!
>   O! Salva nos.

i.e., literally,

> O most high God, save now our King; may his victory
> be happy, and glory his companion; save now our lord.
> O Lord God arise, scatter and curb rebels, confound
> their guile and bring their snares to nought. On Thee
> be our hope fixed. O save us.

There is good reason to think that the "Birthday"
concert-giver may have found this hymn in the library

of the Savoy chapel where he was organist, that it may have lain there since the days of the "Glorious Revolution", and that the King it originally proclaimed was a Stuart. That may be: the only thing we know for certain is that it became public property on December 9, 1743 (new style). Similarly, all that we know of the first two stanzas of the English (practically as they are now) is that they were not made public till soon after May 14, 1744 (new style): that the English is at least five months, and perhaps fifty years, later than the Latin, and we can see for ourselves that it is a close translation. On September 28, 1745, the English version was sung with great enthusiasm at Drury Lane to Arne's accompaniment. The historical events in the light of which the second stanza of the English may be read are (1) Dettingen, July 27, 1743, where George II took the field and defeated the French; (2) Fontenoy, May 11, 1745, where his son lost to them; (3) Preston Pans, October 21, 1745, where Johnnie Cope succumbed to Charles Edward; and (4) Culloden, April 16, 1746, at which Charles's cause was lost. The more placid third stanza was written in October, 1745, when men's minds were beginning to calm down, and the Hanoverian general was saying, "Advise all your friends to buy stocks."

We said that the English was a translation of the Latin. It might, of course, have been the other way; but then it would have been merely a case of somebody doing a copy of Latin verses for no ostensible reason. Besides, if there is anything in the 1688 origin, the Papists would have had their good reasons for the choice of a language in which their religion was couched, and which would not be understood by everybody. Dates therefore become important. When was the *Thesaurus Musicus* published? Chappell's *Old English Popular Music* says "1742(?)". Grove says "1742 or 1743". Julian, "1743 or 1744". The copy in the British Museum has "1743?" and a postcard from the late W. Barclay Squire (17.5.17) tells me that this was because of the advertisement it contained of Oswald's Scotch songs, which were published in November, 1742. They were; but what does not seem to be known to any English investigator is that the music advertised (in this case five pieces) was set out in the reverse order of date, the earliest last, the latest first. Oswald's *Songs* stands last. First, and therefore the latest, stands *Twelve Solos for a German Flute and Bass*: and this is advertised in the *General Advertiser* of May 3, 1744 (old style; May 14, new), as "this day published". The facts are fully set out in Chrysander's article in the *Jahrbuch für musikalische Wissenschaft*, 1863, vol. 1, p. 384.

What we have inherited, then, is a song hammered out under stress of one, possibly of two, great moments in our history. The question was, Under which king? You lifted your glass of wine over your tumbler of water, or you did not. Both sides, in that question, sang, though at different times, this song fervently. The sincerer they were, the more heartily they prayed, in the words of Psalm 68, "rebelles dissipet", or else, "confound their politics", according as they saw in one king or the other the best hope of a stable government. Those who see in *God Save the King* nowadays anything more than a communal aspiration for a stable government under a monarchy lack imagination. It does not ask us with the word "politics" to condemn those who hold other political views, nor with "knavish tricks" to call them knaves. It asks "the Lord that *frustrateth* the tokens of liars" and the God who "hath chosen the weak things of the world to *confound* the mighty", to *scatter* the enemies of a constitutional monarchy and *make them fall.* If an Englishman does not own to that aspiration, all he can do, logically, is to go and live outside the Empire. If he does own to it, he cannot find a better place in which to sing the song which expresses it than a church.

(2) THE TUNE

John Bull, early seventeenth century, wrote something which *may* have been the origin of *God Save the King.* He put no words to it, and he, or rather, his copyist, Mr. Messaus, called it simply "Air". His book disappeared fifty years ago or more, and when it was extant a man called Richard Clark, or, possibly, Dr. Gauntlett, took such liberties with it that we cannot tell whether the C's ought to be sharp or not, though the G's almost certainly are. However, major or minor does not matter much: speaking in decades, most tunes are minor in their 'teens and attain their majority at forty. What does matter is that it is a particular sort of *galliard.*

The Tudor galliard was the merry dance in three-time as opposed to the stately dance in two-time, the pavan. The pavan was so slow that the princess's train could be carried by maids of honour: the galliard so gay that the men made it a point of honour to put in double capers, or to dance their partner so high that, unless she had held her dress down with her hands, her knees would—*Proh! pudor*—have shown. This caper, of either sex, came at the fifth beat of a bar of six. Arbeau, in his *Orchesographie* (year of the Armada), says that the "rest" is utilized by the dancer for a "sault majeur", a spring into the air while the feet twinkle rapidly. Its object is to emphasize " a pose" on the last beat: he calls it "le silence des pieds"; it is "as when a player takes his hands off the virginals for a moment to emphasize the close". That is all very well for dancing, but music likes generally to "keep the motion going", i.e., to fill up rests; so, instead of an actual rest, we have a short note following a long as—

1	2	3	4	5	6
May	he	de	fend	our	laws,
And	ev	er	give	us	cause, etc.

Our English name for galliard is "Sink-a-pace" (= *cinque-pas*, because of the five steps, out of six, that were danced).

We said, a particular sort of galliard; and if you recall the words—and music and dance follow suit—of Michael Drayton's *Agincourt* ("Fair stood the wind for France"), you find four sixes following four sixes (or, which is the same thing, eight threes following eight threes). That is the normal, the classical, galliard. But at the end of the sixteenth century (Barclay Squire once told me) a new dance (or music, or words) was introduced, in which eight followed six. In fact, we can perhaps date it. You remember in *Midsummer Night's Dream* (1594) Quince proposes that the prologue of their play shall be in six and eight, and Bottom (the Conservative) says, "No, let it be in eight-and-eight". And, after all, when the prologue comes, it is in ten-and-ten! So that it is hardly a wild guess to suppose that Shakespeare was making a topical allusion to one of the burning literary questions of the day—Should the dance (poem, harpsichord piece) be in six + eight or eight + eight?—and, having made his point, there was no need for him to carry it out, because the audience have forgotten by that time what the question was. The six + eight seems to have been only a passing fashion—perhaps a caprice of the dancers, for it is dancing that regulates the metre and time of both poetry and music. The great majority of the galliards in the Jacobean and Caroline masques are in eight + eight, and by Purcell's time the thing had died out.

Well, here is the earliest printed version, May 1744, of our national anthem. And no other music which has been suggested as the origin of the national anthem is in that form. When Beethoven said he would show us what a fine tune it was he did not know how fine it had been:

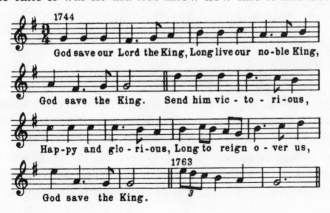

—tune and words exactly as in the original. The barring shown in the words (below) is my suggestion, and if the shape of the tune (differing in bars 1, 4, 5, 13 from what we now sing) is considered, perhaps musicians will accept it; particularly if they reflect that this kind of cross-rhythm at the close of a strain was as much a convention of that age as the simultaneous major and minor sevenths, for a close, had been of Purcell's age. We notice that by 1763 the character had already been taken out of the penultimate bar; the tune simply runs uphill in order to run down again. While it was a folksong the tune improved because it is to the interest of the solo singer to make his song as pointed as he can; but when it was launched on its public career in 1745 at Drury Lane, it gradually deteriorated, because cavalry moves at the pace of the slowest horse. The present tune, though the ruins of a finer, is still fine, and is better adapted to its purpose.

I have a special brief for this 1744 edition because of this fine point of rhythm. The bar of six crotchets—to go back to that—can be taken in two ways—as two threes or three twos. You can sing, either (six-eight)

Long to reign | óver us, Gód save the | king

or (three-four)

Scatter his | énemíes and máke them | fall,

and, what is more, you can sing either of these without feeling that the other is excluded. This is not the Tudor idea of an ending, nor our present practice. It is genuine eighteenth century: Handel (*Messiah*, 1742) was doing it every day, and the *minora sidera* were imitating him. It is a piece of history, and I love it, apart from its being, as it seems to me, aesthetically commendable. Why don't our military bands quietly play *God Save the King* as in 1740, and let the people gradually learn to sing it that way? But they won't, of course.

THE WESLEYS (1)

PERHAPS the reader has by now had enough of music articles, and would think a little sober history a pleasant change; and, for a subject, the Wesley family. Of what the two great brothers, John and Charles, did for religion this is not the place to speak. The family is of interest to us in its relation to poetry and music, and in that connection we can follow it through four generations—grandfather, Samuel; father, Charles; son, Samuel; grandson, Samuel Sebastian. Grandfather and father wrote poetry; son and grandson, music.

It is stretching a point to say that the grandfather wrote poetry. He wrote a great deal, and some of it was in verse; his real contribution lay in having endured with constancy more than his share of misfortune, in poverty, political animosity, and sheer accident; in having chosen an admirable wife who made a real home for a very large family; and in being the father of John and Charles. As a boy he had tramped to Oxford, entered himself at Exeter College, supported himself there, and taken his degree. Beginning with a curacy of £28 a year, being thrown into gaol for debt at thirty-nine (while his parishioners fired his ricks and stabbed his cows), and having his house burnt over his head at forty-three and narrowly escaping (together with the manuscript of his only important hymn, which was found blown into the rectory garden), he died at sixty-nine, leaving the character of an excellent parish priest and a man of ability.

Having had a struggle to find his own, he saw to it that his sons had a good education. Samuel, the eldest, John, and Charles, the eighteenth child, all went to Christ Church, Oxford; John from Charterhouse and the other two from Westminster. Samuel was a High Churchman, politically and theologically, and disapproved, firmly but amicably, of the proceedings of John and Charles; to his family he was all that a good son and brother should be, and he was one of the first promoters of the Westminster Infirmary; he wrote hymns, of course, but few of them have survived. John, the founder of Methodism, was born into a practically heathen England. "Church or no Church," he said, "the people must be saved."

> Those were the days of the war with Spain,
> Portobello would soon be ta'en.
>
> Whitefield preached to the colliers grim,
> Bishops in lawn sleeves preached at him.
>
> Walpole talked of "a man and his price";
> Nobody's virtue was over-nice:—
>
> Those, in fine, were the brave days when
> Coaches were stopped by highwaymen.

Those were the days when George Whitefield's full,

clear, musical voice would reach 20,000 men on a hill-
side, and when 30,000 would wait at 5 a.m. for John
Wesley to come cantering up from some fifty miles away
with his message of hope. John Wesley's idea of the
hymn was that it should be a kind of creed in verse, a
body of practical divinity; and the part he took in the
hymn-books which he edited in great numbers with his
brother Charles was mainly confined to free and fiery
translation from the German.

But Charles approached the hymn as a poet. Not a
public occasion passed—the earthquake panic, rumours
of an invasion, the Gordon riots—nor private—his own
conversion, his marriage, the death of a friend—without
its being the focal point of a number of hymns. He is
said to have written in all 6,500; if that is so, it is one-
quarter of all the original hymns in the English language.
The quality of the best of them is as surprising as the
quantity of the worst. He seemed to have the same
power as his brother of gauging the feelings of average
mankind, and to be able to put them into quite simple
language:—

> Mild he lays His glory by,
> Born that man no more may die

or,

> Those who set at nought and sold Him,
> Pierced and nailed Him to the tree,
> Deeply wailing shall the true Messiah see.

or,

> Other refuge have I none;
> Hangs my helpless soul on thee . .
> Cover my defenceless head
> With the shadow of Thy wing.

or, with a touch of vision,

> Thyself hast called me by my name,
> Look on Thy hands, and read it there!

and of tenderness,

> One army of the living God,
> To his command we bow;
> Part of the host hath crossed the flood
> And part is crossing now.

We know these things so well that we can hardly imagine the revelation they were when there was not much more than metrical psalms for people to sing. Charles Wesley's cheerful friend, G. F. Lampe (for whom Handel had the first double bassoon constructed), wrote some of the tunes; but when such numbers of hymns were being produced—130 each year—to provide distinctive tunes was obviously impossible. It is clear that the old well-known tunes must have been worked hard, and that may partly account for the sameness of our hymn metres. The remaining poet of the family was Charles's sister, Mehetabel (Hetty); her lines have a musical ring about them that reminds us of her brother, and they are unforced, in a way that shows that she was saying what was natural to her. Of the three, Charles alone was happily married. He lived and died in the Church of England, and did not at all approve of John's "ordinations". But all members of the family had a wonderful way of disagreeing entirely on fundamental points without bitterness, and of expressing their views firmly to each other without rancour.

Dean Stanley gave four reasons why poetry applied

to sacred subjects has not had greater success: that
theology, like politics and philosophy, involving argument, is a prosaic subject (but why argue?); that the
greatness of the associations of biblical phrases induces
the writer to ring the changes on them without imparting
a touch of native sentiment or genius (but can native
sentiment always be taken on the lips of a congregation?);
that biblical metaphors lead easily on to anatomical
detail, which again is prosaic if not revolting: and that
few believe themselves equal to writing a treatise on the
stars or a history of the English nation, but many to
treating the truths of religion. Yet, that hymns can be
written we acknowledge every time we sing the glow of
Milton, the terseness of Dryden, the dignity of Cowper,
the pathos of Christina Rossetti, and the miniature of
Herbert. The Wesleys were pioneers. They had few
examples before them except translations, which are a
different matter, and no criticism, except when John
once characterized Charles's Christmas hymns as "namby-
pambical". What Charles thought of John's—

> At this most alarming crisis
>   Shall we not from sin awake,
> While the great Jehovah rises,
>   Terribly the earth to shake?

—is not recorded; but if he was true to himself we may
opine that he did not leave it in obscurity. Prosaic or
fanciful, they put their hearts into the cause.

THE WESLEYS (2)

CHARLES WESLEY, the hymn writer, had two really musical sons, Charles and Samuel; and though people tried to make prodigies of them, the father was content to bring them up properly. Charles picked out tunes at the harpsichord when he was two and a half, and was put under Kelway, the Scarlatti enthusiast, whom Burney praises for "a masterly wildness" at the organ and blames for his compositions, "the most crude, awkward and unpleasant pieces that have ever been engraved". Charles was serious about his music; before playing to anyone, he would ask, "Is he a musicker?" He dabbled in composition, and wrote "fairy melodies"; but that was all.

During his Scarlatti lessons, baby Samuel, nine years younger, would accompany on the back of a chair and, with his back turned to his brother, would cross his hands at the right places as he judged them by ear. Before he was five Samuel had imagined an oratorio, *Ruth*, by singing it over to himself; and at seven and a half he wrote it out as we may read it now in the British Museum. He had taught himself in the meantime how to write notes and words by poring over *Samson*, and his print hand remained with him through life. *Ruth* was sent to old Dr. Boyce, who wrote his compliments and thanks "to Mr. Samuel Wesley, his very ingenious brother composer, and is very much pleased and obliged by the possession of the oratorio *Ruth*, which he shall preserve as the most curious product of his musical library". As the boy grew up he was admired as much

for his behaviour as for his playing. He had what is
rare with musicians, a passion for punctuality, and would
jump off the music stool the moment the clock struck;
when asked if he would go and play to Queen Charlotte,
he said: "With all my heart, but I won't stay beyond
eight." In those days he rose at five; later on he often
went to bed at that hour, because having begun his
composing he wouldn't stop till he finished. Once a
pewter pot of porter was set for him on the hob; next
morning the liquor was found evaporated and the pot
melted. He wrote standing at a high desk, while people
talked or didn't, without blot or erasure. At the organ,
when he was too small to reach the swell pedal, someone
offered to work it for him; but that wouldn't do at all,
so he jumped down and stood where he could reach it.
He did not use the pedal-board, except for occasional
holding-notes: "Let those who can't use their hands play
with their feet", he said.

The brothers made much music together for friends;
Charles seldom had a word to say for himself, Samuel
was fluent and pointed. Charles fancied himself (like
Paganini) on his bow; "this one", he said, as he laid his
hand on his heart, "will do, I think, for the Queen".
When Samuel's portrait, now in the National Gallery,
was painted by Jackson in 1827, his comment was "it's
ugly enough, but it's very like me". When Samuel was
thirteen the boys appeared in public; he astonished
people by his extemporizing on a given theme, and by
transposing "even a fourth". He would also rag Master
Crotch of Norwich, nine years his junior, by mistuning
his violin, and the child always said correctly whether
it should be sharper or flatter. In the year he came of

I

age a tragedy happened. He fell into a deep hole and hurt his head. Wesley-like, he refused to be trepanned; in consequence he was for seven years more than eccentric, and the fit recurred again when he was fifty; these two occasions took a good slice out of his life, for composition stopped *pro tem.*, and he seemed to forget he had ever cared about music.

At the end of the first period somebody (said to be Pinto, but of the two Pintos in Grove one was eight years old in that year and the other eleven years dead) brought him acquainted with J. S. Bach. His ecstasy became an infatuation for "Old Wig", as he called him. It revolutionized his music, as may be seen from a comparison of the rather mild and uneventful Ode on St. Cecilia's Day (1794) with the impetuous 81st Psalm (1800) on a canto fermo, which is taken into all possibly related keys, with the counterpoint running on velvet all the time. (In the English translation "tabouret", which is an embroidery frame, for "tympanum" is a pity; the Bible word "psaltery" might have been kept.)

His more famous son, Samuel Sebastian—for, so fathered and sponsored, what else could he have been called?—was organist in succession of four London churches and four cathedrals (Hereford, 1832; Exeter, 1835; Winchester, 1849; Gloucester, 1865). At the centenary (1910) of his birth seven organists from these churches played. As may be guessed from such a list, he did not get on well with cathedral dignitaries, and there is a thin lip in his portrait at the Royal College that looks rather like that. He was an angler: in London he fished the Commercial Docks; he went to Winchester nominally to educate his sons, but really to fish the

Itchen, and when he was appointed to Leeds (after a difference of opinion at Hereford) he broke his leg fishing the Aire. His music, confined practically to the Church Service is, at its finest, not only far beyond anything of his day, but the best example of the Anglican anthem of any day. Most of the important things are printed, and specimens of the style, adventurous but closely knit, are to be seen in Walker's and the Oxford History. What he understood by the "Church School" is best said in his own words: "It courts no external favour or loud applause, and has no strongly marked rhythm—nothing to quicken the pulsation or excite animal spirits. It bends the mind to devotion, removes all impression of mere sublunary things, and brings home to man an overwhelming sense of his own insignificance and the majesty of the Eternal."

With him the devotion of that family to an art came to an end. That it should have run through four generations is not unexampled, but when it does so, it is a sign of character. Music is a gift, no doubt, and without the gift no one can begin to make it. But the number of musicians who abandon the struggle in early manhood vastly exceeds those who are still battling in middle age, which shows that without strength of will the gift is useless. With the Wesleys the gift was seldom absent, but the strong will was more certainly present.

AN EIGHTEENTH-CENTURY AMATEUR

1. "I have never, from a vain display of erudition, loaded my page with Greek. . . . I have generally had recourse to the labours of the best translators and commentators, or the counsel of a learned friend. And here in order to satisfy the sentiments of friendship, as well as those of gratitude, I must publicly acknowledge my obligations to the zeal, intelligence, taste, and erudition of the Reverend Mr. Twining, a gentleman whose least merit is being perfectly acquainted with every branch of theoretical and practical music" (Charles Burney, *History of Music,* I, xviii, 1776).

2. "The first thing I looked at in your dedication was what you said of me—*c'est la nature.* I held up my fan and looked through the sticks, as Fielding's squeamish lady did. It really looks very well, and it is a very pretty, fat, light, sleek, compact little *éloge;* but it holds a monstrous deal, and I wish it was as near the truth in my mind as, perhaps it may be in yours. But I, who know the man, can only shake my head as I bow it" (Thomas Twining to Charles Burney, January 27, 1776).

IT is curious this mention by Burney of one solitary man who helped him in his work; and one has wondered who he was who deserved this evidently sincere and felt praise. A book by his great-nephew (*A Country Clergyman of the Eighteenth Century,* by Richard Twining, 1882, out of print), which has come into my hands this week, tells us. Burney and Twining had not long been, but were, close friends till the death of the latter in 1804. Burney bustled about in London, on the Continent, collecting insatiably his materials; one can guess partly from his list of a thousand subscribers the sort of people he came across or influenced. There were singers, Agujari (with her C in altissimo), Pachierotti (fancy and flexibility), Farinelli (purity and strength, and that wonderful crescendo), Guadagni (of the *Messiah*); composers, Emmanuel Bach (Sebastian being unknown), Galuppi (Browning's); organists, Boyce (of the *Cathedral Music*), Cooke (of Westminster, writer of catches), Ebdon, of Durham (friend of Ch. Avison, of Newcastle), "Mr." Jackson, of Exeter, Joah Bates (conductor of Handel Commemoration); and other interesting people, such as Sir John Hawkins (the rival historian), William Cowper (who was writing *John Gilpin*), Sir Joshua Reynolds (glad, perhaps, to read about what he was too deaf to hear), Samuel Johnson (who hated music, and thought Dryden's *Ann Killigrew* fine and Gray's *Bard* poor), William Beckford (sowing wild oats preparatory to writing *Vathek*), Daines Barrington (who knew something of Mozart).

And Twining, with ample leisure and a mind as alert as Charles Kingsley's at Eversley, sat quietly all his life at Fordham near Colchester—all except once—his Hegira, he called it—when he migrated to Cambridge, because the Colcestrians in 1803 were in hourly expectation of a French invasion. He was the grandson of Thomas Twining (of Tom's Coffee House, opened 1706 in Devereux Alley), as the present head of the firm is the grandson of his biographer. This book contains letters—too few—between him and Burney, and him and his brother, then head of the firm and the friend of Pitt. His portrait hangs in the board-room—a determined nose, a humorous mouth, kind eyes; and in his letters he knows when he knows, twinkles with fun, loves his friends. He holds up holy hands of horror at the Gordon riots (as Kingsley did *not* at the Chartists), and can't be clear about Louis XVI. But the main thing is the music, with painting and scenery second—"if music is my wife, painting is my concubine". He is a violinist, and it sounds as if he was a good one, for he says of a curate, who has settled near by, that he plays the fiddle (and other things) well. "Now sir, when I say 'well', I can't be supposed to mean the wellness of one who makes those instruments his study; but that he plays in a very ungentlemanlike manner, exactly in tune and time, with taste, accent, and meaning. and the true sense of what he plays." And (with his Stainer, which he exchanges later for a Strad) he speaks of it as "very comfortable fiddling".

In theory he is sound, and Burney owed much of his early chapters to him. There is a good deal he does not understand about Greek music, but the point is, he *knows* he does not understand—and in that form of research there are many who don't. Two things he knows: that the Greeks had no vocal partwriting, but "flung in here and there a common chord or a sprinkle of arpeggio, somewhat like what our old musicians called breaking a ground"; and that, if instruments were employed with acting, "since the instruments could not speak, the actors must sing". (Few will dispute that.) And this is the basis of a view he holds later on: "Mr. —— thinks that vocal performance is good for nothing if the words are not perfectly intelligible. Won't you join with me in absolutely denying this? It seems to me much nearer the truth to say that when the words are perfectly distinct, as in reading, it must be a proof that the music, or the singer, or both, are bad. I have heard Beard [Handel's tenor] commended for this. But was that singing? All this is false musical criticism. Mr. —— wants 'that precise medium which pronounces and sings at the same time'. I say there is no such medium." He heard Sarah Harrop (Joah Bates's betrothed), and had " 'great dispositions to cry'. E —— said he should have cried, if he had not seen how foolish I looked. She sang Pergolesi, Leo, Hasse, from teatime till ten o'clock. She gave me some faint idea of meeting departed friends in heaven." And Pacchierotti. "The voice, not strong, and liable to variation, is to my ear sweet with a peculiar sort of sweetness. In gracing, he does the most beautiful, most unassignable, most unwritten and unwriteable things—no end to his fancy and flexibility. Has faults, though. Sometimes there is a note too flat, or he is too exuberant, wanton; but to have fancy and invention is so rare a fault. His voice needs distance; Burney tells me this is the case with all castratos. He is a conversible creature; loves English, and studies it 'hardly', as he says."

Then composers. "Miserable, hobbling stuff, these smooth airs of Henry Lawes: Purcell, with his old curls and twiddles, is perfection to him." "Lock up your bookcase", he says to a friend, "or I shall come and steal all the Emmanuels I can lay hands on." To Burney (1791), "Tell me about Haydn. F —— told me some quartets had not long ago been published by him [—half of his 83[1] had been published by that date] I am sorry you think I undervalue his 'Stabat'. I allow the merit of

[1] Miss M. Scott discovered an 84th soon after this was written.

quitting his instrumental eccentricity, and getting into
the right style; still, I should have expected more novelty
from him in that style. Some movements are fine, others
appeared to me common, somewhat *passés*. The con-
cluding fugue, in particular, not good in its *genre*; far
below such movements in Jommelli and Pergolesi."
A just judgment. "How does Girowetz go on? [Haydn's
friendly rival, then 28.] That man seems to me to have
something of his own. I look upon it to be, at this time
of day, the most difficult thing of all in music to produce
a piece of melody that shall seem to be new, without
being forced and queer. Now I think I hear such little
bits of felicity, every now and then, in Girowetz's air.
We may fairly call a passage new when it strikes an ear
hackneyed in good melody as, on the whole, uncommonly pleasing. *N'est ce pas?*"

Twining was a man of taste. Of course he was a scholar
and Fellow of his college, Sidney Sussex, and all that.
For the outside world his reputation was based on a good
edition of Aristotle's *Poetics*, which he sent to Heyne,
editor of Virgil, with a chaste Latin letter. He could
hitch Catullus's *Phaselus ille* into English in the
open-hearted way the eighteenth century loved, or write
a letter to a friend in Paris (where he never was) so as to
deceive the Frenchman elect. He had Kingsley's love of
the countryside, but not enough knowledge to write a
Chalkstream Studies, and too much sense to disturb
its peace with a panegyric. He knew his Shakespeare,
and saw the good equally in Swift and in Richardson.
But music was the thing for him. He took it, like Browning, as a metaphor of life; but he loved it too objectively
to have used Abt Vogler (if he ever knew of him) as a

peg for philosophy, and too sanely to have grown sentimental over Avison's March. He could go to a place and
hear, or, with less ease, to a book and read, a piece of
music, form swiftly and securely a judgment on it, and
express that lucidly. They are both difficult things to do.

THE WORCESTER MSS.

THE Chapter Library of Worcester Cathedral contains a volume and a portfolio, both of which are
of interest to musicians.

The volume is a collection of choir books of which
the principal is an antiphoner—a list of antiphons, or
texts to tunes sung before and after each psalm. It is
in at least three hands, and the greater part of it is by the
first hand and written probably in 1230, twelve years
after the last consecration of the cathedral. The antiphoner was almost certainly in use up to 1549, and on
the 23rd of April in that year the service was first read
in the vulgar tongue and all the choir books were taken
to the bishop and burned. This copy escaped; it belonged
to the precentor and was somehow not included with
the rest.

At the end of the sixth century Augustine and his
monks brought Gregorian music to England. This was
soon widely diffused over both the Western Church
and Northumberland in the seventh century. In the
ninth, Alfred, after the Danish invasion, brought over
Grimbault, *cantatorem optimum*, from France and

John the Saxon, of wide learning and trained in music, probably from Corbie on the Somme. There is little doubt that the Gregorian style held its ground during the tenth century in spite of attempts at innovation. The Council of Cloveshoe (747) had condemned the custom by which "secular poetry was babbled (*ne garriant*) in church" and had desired "that the composition and the clarity (*distinctionem*) of the sacred words should not be corrupted or obscured by a dramatic tone of voice (*tragico sono*) and that the melody should be simple and devotional according to ecclesiastical custom"; and if this could not be done the priest was to read the service. In the eleventh century Turstin, the Norman abbot of Glastonbury, wished to introduce from Fécamp a new style of singing, and with armed men proceeded to enforce his ruling; but the monks, after two of them had been killed, seized chairs and candlesticks and drove the soldiers out, and the king had the sense to dismiss Turstin. The Fécamp style against which this stand was made by Gregorian-trained monks was again a question of ornamenting plainsong by "sugary variations (*dulcissimo melodismate*)". There is good reason then for believing that the English church held fast to Gregorian traditions; and it is unlikely that any attempt to upset it would have been made at Worcester, whose Saxon bishop, Wulstan, was the only one whom William the Conqueror continued in his see in 1070.

The portfolio contains fragments on parchment of musical notation of the thirteenth or fourteenth century. A few of these fragments at Worcester contain the plainsong of the Mass, which is easily verified. More are harmonizations in three or four parts. These were described lately by Dom Anselm, O.S.B., to a meeting of the Musical Association, and his lecture was afterwards printed in their Proceedings with examples which could not then, unfortunately, be performed. The following is based on what he said:

The music of to-day is thought of first as music and then, perhaps, as something set to words. But the fourteenth century, starting with the liturgical words and tunes, embellished these by the composition of other words, which it called a Trope, and of other music, which it called either Motet or Conductus. The *Trope* is explained in *The Winchester Troper*, 1894, by Dr. W. H. Frere, now Bishop of Truro, as the interspersing in divine service of vocal music, originally without words, in connection with some liturgical piece. It is spoken of by Augustine as "jubilation (*qui jubilat non verba dicit, sed sonus quidam est laetitiae sine verbis*)". From the tropes sprang lauds, sequences, proses and the like. The trope (which had words eventually) was followed by a jubilation (without words), but this becoming unduly extended could not (in the absence of notation) be remembered without words, which accordingly were added, and the addition was called a sequence or a prose; instances of these are in the Worcester fragments. The word *Motet* is connected by some with the French *mot*, Latin *mutire*, a derivation which gains support from the fact that the voices all sang different but relevant "words"—for instance, different hymns in honour of the Virgin. By others it is referred to *motus*, and indeed the parts generally "moved" in contrary directions, or to *mutatus*, for they did in fact embellish or "change" the tenor (the lowest voice); and the early form of the word, *mutetus*, lends colour to this. (Later forms, *motectus* and *motettus*, may have something to do with the Italian printer and his & and tt). The early motet had its three (or four) voices on two facing pages, in front of which the singers stood. In the fine sixteenth-century printed choir-books, similarly set out by Gardano and Petrucci, the 4, 5, 6 and more voices sing the same words, but that possibility had not occurred to the fourteenth century; it came in with the *Conductus*, and is implied in the name. Here the text is written over the lower voice and sung by it, while the upper voices vocalize on the prominent vowel sound (and in Latin the agreement of noun and adjective generally produces one). The whole is written in score and the parts move, with imitations and breaks between the phrases, in the same direction.

The historical value of these fragments is that they help to fill the gap between the Reading Rota (1226) and the Agincourt Song (1415), and to dispel the myth that counterpoint began in this country with Dunstable (b. 1445). Their musical value is not small, for they will, when they have been deciphered, tell us more of the practice of the art at that time than we know, for instance (in the absence of any clue to the rhythm), of ancient Greek music from our ten precious fragments. They show as yet nothing on the level of Reading but they contain measured rhythms (as opposed to the verbal rhythms of plainsong), a shifting of the melody from one part to another and even fugal entries.

For the creed that music must have a purpose beyond itself other creeds have now begun to be substituted—that music is self-expression, that it is decoration, or that it takes the place of religion. This last, the only one of the three which is tenable in the long run, means that music is its own purpose. Not that beauty is in a general way identical with goodness, but that a definite change has come about in music itself. Then, music was not yet independent of words, and those words were inevitably religious because in religion was wrapped up all the knowledge that men possessed in common. But now, music fares equally well with and without words, and moreover, knowledge pours in upon us from a hundred different sources, so that our question is, Where are we to find a common stimulus of feeling? For if, as has been said, beauty is born of attention, it would seem that as knowledge is increasingly differentiated attention has its chance only when we specialize; and that, rather than sigh for a lingua franca in which to address the universe, we ought to be content to talk in our own dialect— theatrical, choregraphic, choral, orchestral, or liturgical —each composer to his own particular audience; not, in fact, that religion is incapable of taking again the position it once held, but that the day of universal geniuses is over.

No doubt we specialize more, but our several speciali- zations still need a unifying principle. If formal religion no longer holds the place it did, it does not follow that religion is dying out, nor that religion, if it is here among us, is unable to inspire a common feeling. It may even be the stronger for not being hampered by too much for- mality. In spite of some appearances to the contrary the prayer of the Churches for unity is perhaps being granted in a larger way than they expected, by the *consensus* of the ethical opinions and judgments of right-thinking

men and women, and religion by broadening its basis
may have gained in both intellectual and emotional force.
If that is so, what more could music ask? Fifty years
ago R. L. Nettleship, the philosopher, wrote—thinking
chiefly of Schubert and Brahms, for he was a singer
—that music seemed to him to be almost the only reasonable form of religion. We may quote also (from memory)
a phrase from the opening prayer at the Three Choirs
Festival: "Almighty God, Who hast ordained that the
hearts of men are moved by the sound of music and their
minds thereby attuned to the understanding of Thy
mysteries . . .", and we know that this prayer embraces
within its sanction much that is not specifically religious
music. If we bring Walt Whitman or Binyon or whoever
it may be into church, we feel that we are not "babbling"
them in the sense which the eighth century condemned,
but substituting new metaphors for old about the things
which words never wholly express. And where words
stop music begins, as many have felt besides Wagner,
who said it. Music does not take the place of religion;
it cannot tell us what we believe but it does tell us how
much we believe it. After all, what, in principle, is the
oratorio but a Trope, the old symphony but a Jubilation,
and the new symphony (with voices) but a Sequence,
in some service that takes place, it may be in a church,
but certainly in our hearts?

NATIONAL ART

IT is proposed to say a word here, not about National Anthems, which are flags, flown on State occasions, of high emotional value, nor about "national" songs, which are specific statements of what the nation generically feels on a lower plane, or is supposed to feel—thoughts on roast beef, on ripe cherries, or on crossing the Bay of Biscay; nor about "traditional" songs, adored by infancy, despised by manhood, and treasured by eld that has tasted all the flavours and finds this one the most satisfying of them all. Those will do perhaps for some other day, but to-day we will consider two previous questions—whether there is any art which is not in the first instance national, and, how a nation that has not got art may hope to get it.

Because art has before now spelt itself with a capital, and worn its hair long, or carried a lily in its hand, there is no need for a healthy mind to be afraid of it. Art is the doing in an uncommon way of what most people do in a common way. Anybody can hack a duck when it comes on the table, a few can carve it; and the man who can lay on the plate a leg intact or clean slices of the breast we call, to that extent, an artist. Many people can make shift to tell a story; but we keep the name of artist for the man who can find the right word for the thing, who does not waste time, who holds a dramatic balance, and who knows his subject well enough to play with it.

A national art of music is the singing well of thoughts which people who speak the same language are able to say well. That principle is not weakened by the fact that they may go on to write symphonies and tone-poems, which have no words; for though the voice cannot sing these, the heart can, and they are not good music unless it does. Some of us can speak Italian or write Latin, but it is obvious that we do not know those languages well enough to dream in them; it ought to be equally obvious that when we adopted the manner of Mendelssohn and Brahms, we were not writing true music, nor are we now if we are content to pick up wrinkles from Stravinsky and Hindemith. *Wess das Herz voll ist, dess geht der Mund über.* We are apt to think of opera and symphony as the property of Western civilization. They are not; they are what various men, born in Central Europe in 1732, 1756, 1770 and 1813, when they came to ripe years, felt in their heart of hearts. All true art is national in that sense; and to say that German music is logical, French thrifty, and Italian graceful, is to say that it was made in a time and a place where those virtues, among others, were laid to heart, alike by the common and the uncommon men.

Nations succeed then, by their positive virtues, not by mere absence of vices, nor by the presence of other people's virtues; in that they are very much like individuals. And art, faithfully holding the mirror up to nature, records that success in its own medium. What kind of success has this nation had? That is for others to say, but we may say what we have tried to do, and that is, in two words, to play fair. We begin it in games, which have been filling our spare afternoons for a couple of centuries (and when anyone begins to play them on some other principle, we have half a mind to

. . . but, well, we don't, because we are too fond of them).
We carry it on into our law and politics and colonization,
and it is to be seen any day in the policeman who is a
good citizen or the citizen who is ready on any emergency
to wear a badge on his arm. What we fundamentally
desire is to pull together, and we not seldom achieve it.
Hence, when we have desired to make music, it has
usually been choral. Our Festivals show us how that
comes about. Music is pent up in underground lakes all
over this country, waiting for the right man to come and
give it an outlet to "valleys of springs of rivers". In
choral music everyone has an equal chance of helping,
without the invidiousness of being conspicuous; and
that suits us, who are at heart amateurs and want to leave
the science of the thing to experts.

And what do other peoples say of us? They say
our music is "pastoral". That strikes us as odd, because
we think of ourselves as rather well informed and up
to date. But there may be some truth in it. Which nation
has had the best water-colour school? Which makes
most fuss about the desecration of the countryside?
Which first photographed birds and beasts instead of
shooting them? Does our lyric poetry, no meagre
achievement in bulk or quality, ever tire of country
sights and sounds? And so it comes that, if we write,
we write a sort of landscape music, for that is the strand
that, more than any other, seems to run through the
work of all our composers; it was to be heard very
obviously in Mr. Bliss's new clarinet quintet. Opera
and symphony may be beyond us; in neither have
we yet reached world fame; ours proceed rather from
other people's virtues than from our own. But we

K

have written music called by those names, and these betoken the eye for scenery, the delight in variety and adventure, and the love of "the quietest places under the sun".

NEW WORKS

VAUGHAN WILLIAMS: THE PASTORAL SYMPHONY

VAUGHAN WILLIAMS's Pastoral Symphony differs from its two predecessors, and from every other symphony, chiefly as being cast throughout in one mood. Three of the four movements are *moderato* and the slow movement is *andantino*; the Scherzo alone has livelier moments, but they are shortlived. It looks on paper as if relief from monotony had been sought in the "scansion" of the themes, which is extremely various; but the effect of this when we hear it is only to abolish any salient rhythm. Moreover, there are few pronounced climaxes, and there is the opposite of a climax at the end of each movement. The composer has deliberately denied himself, therefore, all the ordinary aids to structure, and relies entirely upon what we are fain to call the "poetry" of the music—the setting of his subject-matter in imaginative surroundings, and forcing it to give up more and more of its meaning at each of its many recurrences. That is, perhaps, why he chooses themes which are diatonic, or not even that. He will have nothing but the barest statement, no adornments and no compromise.

131

The statements are often quite bald. The least intangible is the theme of the Scherzo, and that is merely the last three bass notes of any piece of music from the sixteenth century onwards. The themes, that last refuge of the analytical critic, are here only those roots and vertebrae which Nature buries out of sight. Nature has no climaxes, no patterned rhythms, no pathetic moments; man adds all these when he looks at her. And this music is to hold the mirror up to Nature. The country, the country of England, "a country of deep pasture and quiet downs and earthy fields, where the furrows run straight from hedge to hedge". How this is to be got into tones we do not know; the tones are such that they allow us to think it, and, thinking it, we understand the tones better. The sounds of the countryside are beautiful, not in themselves, but as enriched by association and poeticized by inference; the proof is that spring astonishes us each year more, not less. Music, if it is to use association, must not be afraid to repeat, and if its inferences are to be striking, the clashes must be bold. Both must be meant, and strongly meant, and the good composer means them. And as there are composers to whom a primrose is a yellow primrose—and, if nothing more, yet perfect at that—such as Mozart, so there are others to whom, as to Beethoven, it can give thoughts too deep for tears. Vaughan Williams is one of those to whom tones give not ecstasy but "thoughts"—not the arguments of the thinker but the long thoughts of the child. His music does not answer questions; it asks them. It takes the questioner aside, and says to him: "This is what you meant to ask, isn't it? It's just what I want to know myself." And, in doing that, it gives all the answer the question will bear.

No painter has left clearer brushmarks than this composer; every phrase cries aloud, for good or ill, who made it. Like one of them in particular, he stands back and paints with a long brush from the place from which he intends his picture to be looked at; like him, too, he has had his Herrera and his Pacheco for teachers, and yet has remained self-taught; like him, again, he has learnt his art among the common things of life, and sees the uncommon things not as idealizations of those but as superstructure on a truly laid foundation. It is the difficult way both for composer and for listener, this of avoiding obvious beauty in order to get unexpected strength. It is easy to start from some vantage point inaccessible to most, and make short and daring excursions where few can follow. It is hard to start from the homesteads in the valley and reach the heights by sheer ice-craft and weather-wisdom. The great music of the world has always done this; and when we lose interest in the classics, as by constant repetition we must, it is partly because we do not know altogether where they started or what their problems exactly were; and if we did, we should not call them classics. To which remark the reader may append his own corollary.

Yet if the symphony is difficult to give oneself any account of, it is easy to feel sure about. For the first time, if we may say so, we have no qualms about the mastery of technical difficulties, no suspicion that the weight of the subject-matter exceeds the power to express it, no consciousness of a machinery between us and the music. Whether it is the lapse of time since the *London* or what has happened in that time, there is a difference both in the touch and the vision. The *Pastoral*

begins another "manner"; and when we reflect that
Vaughan Williams is still in the prime of life, our gratitude for this is tempered only by hopes of what may
yet be.

CHRISTMAS

WHO has ever thought of using music to make the
English Christmas a dramatic thing? Plays, yes,
miracle plays; and dancing, carols (if etymology is any
guide); and mummery, now fallen into decrepitude.
But music? Well, yes, there is Vaughan Williams's
Fantasia on Christmas Carols, but he would not call that
dramatic exactly: it is the carol, not as we imperfectly
sing it, but as musicians idealize it, the counterpoints
they hear in it and want to express whenever they can
get the opportunity; so he gives them one. But here is
someone who looks steadily at Christmas as an event,
spiritual and social, historical and pathetic, and asks
himself what music has to say to *that*.

His name is Benjamin Britten, and what he writes is
called *Choral Variations*. Variations on what? On
Christmas, of course. Nominally, they are on a "German
XVIth century" something, and that is in fact pro-
pounded and referred to, but the variations discuss all
manner of things for which it does not give chapter and
verse. Jesus was a Baby; that is the first thing we think
about him. We must not disturb him because he has
come a long journey, poor little mite, or his mother

who is very tired, so we sing "Lullay", and go on singing it over and over again, a little more gently as he dozes off. When he is asleep we have time to think of what has happened, to bring a baby to a caravanserai where he has to be put to bed in a draughty manger. It was that Herod! Herod! we howl: Herod, a thoroughly respectable king, no doubt, but, seen from this angle, a monster. Then we turn to the babe again and look at him lying there, quite unconscious of his wrongs and of our indignation, and lift up our voice in prophecy; we see into the future twenty centuries hence and call him our Saviour; and the boys (who are the shepherds, of course) a little aside, unable to see so far, murmur musically, "Jesu! Jesu!"

Then the Three Kings come, busy and preoccupied with the importance of the moment; fussing a little— we hear their pattering feet in the bass—but gradually infecting all minds with their enthusiasm, and lifting all hearts by their understanding and humility. And what a time for them to have come! Everything bound in frost and iron. The hard ring of feet on the cobbles outside, the splitting, shivering sound of the ice as it cracks on the roof. We hear these in the ruthless semitones that trebles and altos hold against one another, that many may have thought, but that no one has had the wit to write; and here it is, as easy as lying. Harmony is logic, but at Christmas logic goes to the winds. Therefore we sing in semitones, because they are the bitter truth of the moment, and obey some higher law of harmony that we have not yet learnt.

Last, the finale: and what more shall we say? What is the ultimate truth of Christmas, not for the philosophers

but for Everyman? Well, it is a birthday and it is good
cheer; so we sing Noel! and Wassail! till our throats are
dry. They are the epitome of all we have been singing,
in a piece of music that is as long as *Jesu, meine Freude*
and, in a different way, has filled us with as much elation.
And when we have no more Noel! left in us, we just
prattle semi-audibly to our neighbour about his sheep
that were out in the November floods, about his carter
and whether he has given him another chance, the
fairings he got for his wife, and what not; and then
with "Glory to God and jolly mirth" put on an equal
pedestal—because they are so—we bring in Christmas.

That is a rough outline of what I heard at the Mercury
Theatre recently. You may not know the place
because the name has lately been changed from "The
Ballet Club", a minute from the Notting Hill Gate
stations. It was an evening of first performances: Miss
Dorothy Gow's string quartet, in one movement (quite
short, and repeated), with a theme of the kind that leaves
one gaping, but well-proportioned; Alan Frank's Suite
for two clarinets, a series of short epigrams; and Arnold
Cooke's Quintet for harp, flute, clarinet, and two
strings, compact of stumpy phrases and contrapuntal
at all costs, but merry withal. Madame Kortchinska's
harp was a strengthening element, and Miss Lemare's
handling of the variations was as clear and intelligent
as any I have yet heard from a feminine conductor.
The main thing is that it is worth a great deal to have
a place in London where English compositions that do
not involve great expense have a reasonable chance of
being heard.

A word about the choir of thirty. They do not give

themselves a name, and they ought not to, of course, because they are friends who have just looked in for Christmas, unless they are relations who believe in keeping the family together. They enjoyed what they were doing, and that is three parts of the whole. But besides that they knew very well what they had to do; they took their points, and they kept pitch. One would guess—though no one can tell who does not actually sing in it—that it was not altogether easy music. To sing fifty or so Noels on end, even when handily divided among the different voices, asks some endurance. But the parts are so vocal, and the substance and intent so clear, that no one need be fainthearted about it. So altogether these *Choral Variations* are quite a thing for any musician-like choir to make a note of for 1935.

And a word about the composer; not his personality, of which I know nothing, but his music, which tells us all we need to know. It has one mark of mastery—endless invention and facility. He takes what he wants, and does not trouble about what other people have thought well to take. He rivets attention from the first note onwards: without knowing in the least what is coming, one feels instinctively that this is music it behoves one to listen to, and each successive moment strengthens that feeling. He inspires confidence; there is no wondering what is coming next; whatever that may be, and whether we "like" it or not, we shall agree with it.

CRITICISM

DAY-TO-DAY MUSIC

FRAGMENTS OF A LETTER TO ONE WHO ASKED
HOW TO SET ABOUT BECOMING A MUSICAL CRITIC

THE subject has to be found in the room. It is somewhere in the music played or somewhere in the performer. But it is not these, exactly. It is something you
bring to them. Somebody once said we ought never
to read a book without asking ourselves first what questions we expected to have answered in it. The trouble
is that we never know what we want to ask till we hear
one or two of the answers, and then our questions are
too many to write down, and so we just read on. A book
diary is not a bad thing—just an account of what interested us and what we still want to have explained.
That is roughly what a series of concert notices is.

But there is another difficulty. Whom are we writing
for? It is impossible to write for no one in particular.
Is it for someone who was there or someone who was
not? Does he know much or little about music? I have
a man in my mind's eye, for whom I write, a great friend

of mine. I never know whether he is present in the room or not, so that question settles itself by never being settled. Is he musical? Yes, and no. He is always maintaining his ignorance, and deferring to the opinion of those who, he says, know. But over a long period I have never found him wrong, I mean hopelessly wrong, on the important matters. He has quite clear and firm opinions on things, but a unique way of expressing them. If he likes a thing he makes a joke about it, for fear he should stifle it with praise, and if not, he changes the subject with some skill. I am not sure there is any better way of writing a concert-notice.

You agree that there's no harm in changing the subject when the thing won't do at all, but why not say a thing is good, you ask, when it is good? It is all a matter of scale. There was a wonderful teacher of the classics at Charterhouse, who when a good construe of Horace was risked, as boys do risk sometimes in an unconscious sort of way, used to say, "Not so bad"— never anything more. They used to speak of him with affection and bated breath. Grown people are much like boys, and when they risk a good thing they generally do it unconsciously too, and then, if they are the right sort, the best thing to do is not to make a fuss about it but allow it to put you in a good humour, and to show that by a general festivity; if they are not, it does not matter much what you say. But most people are, and anyhow it is best to assume that they are.

There is also a minor difficulty in the way of effusive praise. Most of the laudatory words in the English language have been worked to death, and no amount of very's, really's, thoroughly's, wonderfully's and the

rest, will bring back breath to their lifeless bodies.
And there were very few of them to start with, because
we do not coin them much. We get along in ordinary
speech as best we can with "ripping" and "jolly decent"
and "tophole", and anything more sober sounds stilted.
However, the loss is not great; we shall provide so much
less for the advertisement-mongers, that's all.

Let's get back to "the subject". It is not in the music
or the performer, but in something you bring to them.
At first you will say you have nothing much to bring.
There is your whole musical past, which is a good deal
more than you think. But it is not yet accessible to you.
You haven't had practice yet in thinking things over
and seeing their bearings. You haven't got your instances
ready yet or, what is more important, the habit of mind
that sees the telling points in the new instances. But to
grow that habit of mind is one of the pleasures of living.
We all criticize—which only means, judge—people
and things every day and all day; it is the salt of life,
and all we can hope to do is gradually not to be like
old Tulliver, "mistook in his jedgments". This "something you bring", or will bring, is the "habit of thinking
things over". After we have heard a piece of music
that is new to us we don't for the moment know what to
make of it. Our ideas haven't yet had time to sort themselves out. After a little time, spent perhaps in thinking
of other things, we come back to it and find that our
dominant feeling about it is that it was fresh, or enter-
prising, or fanciful, or poetical, or logical, or consistent,
or faithful to type, or what not. The dominant feeling
is the important thing, because it is probably right,
and probably the only thing we can hope to be right

about at a first hearing. Having settled this we find the music falls into a class and we may happen to think of another composition like enough to be worth comparing or contrasting with it. Then, our general idea must have been based on particulars, of which we can probably remember one or two enough to describe them a little. Clever people will be able to say more than this, but the average man will not; and it is enough. It is futile for anyone to expect epoch-making decisions hot and hot with next morning's coffee and rolls: they are simply not to be had, and decisions are anyhow best left to time.

The more important matter is how you put it; right or wrong—and both eventualities must be contemplated —you want people to read you, and to tell their friends that they take in the *Midday Advertiser* chiefly for the music. The surest way to be read is to write as you would talk (with synonyms for "tophole" and the others). Within limits that can be done. The chief limit is that intonation of voice is to count for nothing; so if a word has, at all costs, to be stressed you must adopt some dodge like the comma after "has" in this sentence. To write as you talk you must know pretty well what you are going to say, and then dash it down, taking a risk or two. Your editor will probably help with the graver risks. I remember writing "get" (which in the circumstances was a little bit slangy) and, lower down, "infection" (which strained a metaphor to the breaking-point), and an ingenious man altered them for me to "yet" and "inflection", making in each case rather better sense, without their being to the author's *amour propre* anything more than misprints. We can't expect to get all the balls over the net, but we may win without it, and anyhow what the spectators want is hard service and a quick volley. If I know you, that is the kind of thing that will suit you, as you are not the kind of person who uses ten words where five would do.

But, in another way, writing is different from talking. In talking we can correct or modify our statements, but in writing we are practically making a will, in the sense that people we never heard of will have nothing but our words and our stops to enable them to decipher our meaning. It is best, in that case, to imagine ourselves to be addressing not only our good friend, but also our friend the enemy—one who is going to take everything exactly as we didn't mean it. He owes you no grudge, of course, but you are simply an anonym to him, and so there is no need for him to stand on ceremony. In this predicament some writers take refuge in journalese, a kind of book-making by double entry, where everything is said twice over in hopes that one of the ways will neutralize the other in case it was wrong. It was possibly for this defect that the Indian Government lately sent 10,000 files to the burning ghauts, if I am correctly informed. The remedy is not to mean two things by whatever you say, but to say one thing that you mean, and, as a corollary, not to say it unless you mean it.

Well, the best thing, no doubt, is to be oneself, but there is no one to whom the personal equation becomes so tiring after a time. We read Mr. Newman his ingenious paradoxes and Mr. Harvey Grace his genial and open-eyed optimism, and all these wonderful fellows, and wonder how it is they manage to keep finding new handles to old things that we never thought of, and can be light-hearted where we were so solemn, and, worst of all, so like ourselves. We never get a holiday from our own prepossessions.

I am not quarrelling with your view if I simply state mine. The bottom problem in discussing music is to say what "life" is (in it). We don't get any nearer by calling it *psych*-anything, because *psyche* "is" simply life. I regard the musician (the composer first, but others afterwards) as just a *man functioning*. Man may function physically (deeds, mimes, etc.) or mentally (words, tones, etc.); and, of course, there is no *physis* without a little *mens*, and vice-versa. When Hindenberg or Foch order a certain disposition of troops we may say, if we like, that they are expressing an emotion, but I prefer to say that they are functioning—doing that which all their past experience has fitted them for, upon which they have specialized. So Holst and Vaughan Williams, and any others that count. We may say that "Mars" strikes terror, or the beastliness and splendour of it all, or the nobility or futility, or what not, may come before us suddenly; perhaps it does—but that is mainly because it is called "Mars," and because we have just been through what we suppose to have been an unusually repulsive form of war. All that has happened really is that Holst is very much alive, and says so, and we rejoice at the fact; or, in more technical words, that he has found a large enough canvas for his pedal points and driving rhythms, and can show himself as he really is, and not as those four songs for voice and violin only half show him—that he is functioning "to some tune", in fact. Music does what it does for us listeners not by playing upon, or even merely expressing for us, our emotions, but as a health-giver: it "interests" us, it makes us feel very much "in" it, and suddenly aware how trivial are most of the things with which we fill up the day; it makes us alive, makes us feel what it would be to function properly—i.e., good stuff does, and we are not talking of any other.

As to whether, in doing this, music addresses itself more to the intellect or the feeling, I should say that depended on which of the two the maker or the recipient had cultivated most. All women, and 33 per cent of the men, have given the preference to the emotional side, and 67 per cent of musical criticism should accordingly be addressed to the emotions.

As to what the act of creation actually is, I hold that it is ultimately the act of naming. "This", said Adam in the Garden of Eden, "is a lion: a lion let him be." " 'And this', said M. R. F." (in *Dombey & Son*, isn't it?), " 'is a little pillar of the Church.' " And a lion and a pillar of the Church they remain to this day. "This", says Holst, in "Mars", "is how sorry you feel when you think of unavailing jangle and pitilessness, and exactly how sorry you didn't know before I told you, though there are plenty of other things to be sorry about, as I may show you some day when chance brings them up; but the point is not so much which particular sorrow as how much of ourselves you and I can get into it, how much we can function, live life."

LETTERS TO LISTENERS

THESE letters are rewritten from notes made at the time. If any correspondent recognizes his own, I hope he will not think that, with the names and general style altered, undue liberties have been taken with it.

To Mrs. Britain, The Old Grange, Lower Fiddleworth

Thank you for your most kind letter. . . . About the "new music" on the wireless—you say you have given it a good try, and it does not seem to become any more intelligible than at first; and I quite understand; in fact, you are not alone in that. But if I may say so, music is made up of many different things, some of which wireless cannot reproduce. We hear the applause, for instance, and the coughs, but, not seeing either players or audience, we cannot judge either effort or effect. When we are sitting in our own room, the new music seems to come at us without any handle to catch hold of it by, and we find ourselves staring into the loud-speaker, as if that would help; whereas, with the *Egmont* overture, we can shut our eyes in order to be able to *see* the down bows of the fiddles at the A flat place and the second flute take up his piccolo for the coda.

But in the room itself the new music is by no means easy. We catch ourselves thinking something like this:—

Well, they're off. That's not difficult, anyhow. Yes, I expect he means to . . . Oh, no, he's going that way; it'll do just as well . . . Now I'm lost! (I wish that man wouldn't rustle the programme.) . . . There's that bit

L

again . . . and that queer chord. (Oh, why do people
bring children to concerts!) And now he's getting a lift
on. I must hear this! . . . Great stuff! Good man! . . .
Queer ending, though. . . . Oh, no, there's more of
it. . . . This is something like! (I see X—— over there
lapping it up too) . . . but a little disjointed, isn't it?
Still, it sounds like his own, doesn't remind me of anyone.
Give him an a—! Let's look at the programme note. "The
scene is laid in Northern Spain. It is Corpus Christi day,
and the villagers are carrying the image of the Virgin
up into . . . A procession of monks is heard chanting
the . . . Suddenly, a party of brigands, attired in . . ."
But this must be some other piece; or, if it isn't, what do
we want to know all this for anyhow?

It is terribly unsatisfactory, I'm afraid, but if people
spoke truth, this is about all that they actually do hear
at first. *L'appétit vient en mangeant*, and then it gets
easier. With old music we know how the thing is done;
here we do not, and there is a certain charm in that.
Also, we have to judge these things for ourselves:
other people's opinions are of very little use to us. And
I don't think we are necessarily fools if we can't make
up our minds for a long time.

To a cousin, late of Holy Innocents College, Oxbridge

Dear Archie,—Can't I "wake up those people and
get them to put less stale things into their programmes"?
I don't know who "those" people are, and I can't get
at them. Also, like some other people, you overrate the
power of the Press: the Press is the flywheel, not the
engine—supply the "power", and it'll see that every

machine in the factory gets its share of it, but it can't start things. But what is it that you call stale? The classics generally? The well-known classics? Anything before 1900? Anything you've heard twice—or once? I expect you're a "first-performance" man. Well, whichever it is, the answer's pretty much the same. Look at my dog. There are only three decent walks I can take round about here, varied by certain short or long cuts. He runs free; less intelligent dogs go on a lead. He knows these three by heart, because he waits at the cuts to see which it's to be, and it's surprising what a lot of interest he finds: a road up, where he can scratch; a street accident he can fetch me to see; a child's lost ball, treasure trove; besides those delicious smells, all but two or three of which are beyond me entirely. After a hundred hearings of the *Meistersinger* overture, I may still any day hear something new in it. I'm all with you for a brand-new thing now and then, and the grind of following it, and wondering what it's at; and I should agree in wishing that there could be a holocaust of all copies of Liszt's sonata, if it weren't for its historical interest. But on the whole the best sort of world is the one that it takes all sorts to make.

I hope the fiddle's going strong. I'm sending the Bach sonatas you said you hadn't got; the root of the matter's there. We've got a pf. quartet in the house now— Mary, and Mr. Stimson's 'cello, and I write out the second violin parts for Tony's clarinet. The neighbours have said nothing—as yet.

To a Hostess

. . . Yes, I've often wondered. One doesn't want
to clap, and turn a drawing-room into a concert-hall;
nor to discuss other things by the same man, which may
seem as if one was displaying knowledge, or possibly
lead to their being played as well when the programme is
already long enough; not to say "marvellous!" which
isn't true; nor "very interesting!" which is patronizing;
nor "whose is it?" which might imply undesirable
ignorance. Isn't attention the best form of thanks? A
player feels that at once; it makes everything worth
while, and he does his best. And when he does that,
there may be some bit he plays extraordinarily well,
and you notice it; and then it's easy to say "I liked"—
don't say "I loved"—that bit where (or just before,
or after) the hands crossed (or the electric fused, or
Papa came in), making a suggestive curve in the air
with a trailing thumb; and he'll understand, and hum it,
and sit down feeling it really was rather a success.
However, as you say, all the cases are different; still,
I think the main thing is to attend, really attend; though
what attending means, or might mean, I've been trying
all my life to find out.

To Miss Psyche Lovejoy

My Dear Young Lady,—You ask a very difficult
question. It has troubled the world since Job xxxviii. 7,
to know what music "means", and it will still be troubling
it when we come to the four chapters that begin with
Rev. viii. 6, when we hope that, and many other things,

will be made plain. But you don't want all that—in a letter! I will answer your question by another. Of what else that we think beautiful, besides music, do we ask "what it means"? We don't of a face, for instance; or, if we did, it would be no answer to say that the deep-set eyes meant thought and the firm-set chin character, and so on; the face is just that face, and that's all about it. But that is Nature, I hear you protest, and we are talking of art. Still, there too, we don't ask the "meaning" of Salisbury Cathedral, of the Piccadilly Eros, of the Sistine Madonna, of Milton's *Hymn on the Nativity*; why should we ask it of the "*Unfinished*" *Symphony*? It might be said that Eros was the god of love, and that the hymn was about divine love being made human, and the Madonna the type of the best kind of human love; whereas the cathedral and the symphony—well, you couldn't say what they were "about". But look at those first three again; take the poem, as the easiest to discuss without examples. Why is it better than an ordinary Christmas carol, which tells the same story—a story, moreover, that we know without the telling? It is better because the story—which is just that story, though it might have been another—doesn't really matter; whereas the exaltation and vista and justness of thoughts-in-words does matter very much. And the symphony only goes one stage further; there is no story, except what foolish people sometimes invent; the vista is everything, only those people cannot "hear" it. So, if I may suggest, set all you know of carols or any other songs humming in your head, and see if you can't hear how the "*Unfinished*" betters them all; and then it will be clear to you that it doesn't mean this or that story, but the story-without-an-end that is behind them all. Browning, whom I see you read, didn't mean that "we musicians know" the answers to riddles that have stumped financiers or theologians, but that we (including them, very likely) have an answer to their case, because ours fits every case that could be invented.

To Lt.-Col. M. A. Bright, Punjab Army, retired

My Dear Colonel,—Of course I remember you, as a choir treble, and your nickname, which I won't insult you with now. . . . You want music to have a practical bearing on human affairs, not to be so much up in the air. You don't mean, I suppose, that it should be a kind of audible flag, like *See the Conquering Hero* or *O Rest in the Lord*, where the words first said the thing and the music then spelt it out at the masthead; but an audible decoration, something to correspond to flowers or bunting, as we may use things like the march in Parry's *Birds*, or in Mackenzie's *Sayid*. Of course there are heaps—*Peer Gynt*, overture to *Figaro*, or *Lohengrin*, Act 3, bits of Franck and Sinding, Volkmann and Reinecke— Hollywood has lists, no doubt, to show what they all "register". But wouldn't you say that the times when Anglo-Saxons have made less than others of music have been those when they persisted in thinking of it as cut flowers for table decoration, instead of as growing in a garden?

What you really mean is, I think, that you want more light music. So do we all, but we want it good, and there isn't enough to go round. I never can see why a good many of Beethoven's finales shouldn't be used—

the Fourth Concerto, for instance, or the Eighth Symphony. That was the human thing about him, that he could write both kinds. Only I wouldn't *apply* them to "human affairs", but just have 'em for their own sweet sake; and I wouldn't in the least mind detaching them (some, not all) from their context, because they sit quite lightly to it. He has said his real say in the other movements, when we were fresh and attentive, and now he's saying good-bye with a jest on his lips.

AMATEUR AND PROFESSIONAL

Arthur duke coleridge, born 1830, Eton and King's, was a nineteenth-century musical amateur of the best type. His business was the Bar, his leaning towards religion, his respect for those who preached or practised it, his admiration for those who did both. He had a genius for friendship, a passion for music, and a light tenor, of which Walmisley said: "You have the voice of an angel, and can't sing one d—n"—a defect which he set to work to remedy until he could appear without disgrace on the same platform as Jenny Lind. With her and her husband he had a hand in bringing about the first performance of the B Minor in 1876, in which they sang the *Domine Deus* together. He writes in his *Reminiscences* (Constable, 1921):—

> No artist of her time more keenly rejoiced in that great revival than did dear Mme. Golschmitt. I remember her saying to me. "To think that an old woman like me

(she was fifty-six), who have lived in music all my life, should have to be told of this music by an amateur!"
. . . She trained the soprani and alti, and enrolled herself in the choir. . . . A few words that fell from Professor Walmisley in 1849 had lodged in my mind, to the effect that the noblest choruses ever written by man were in a work whose existence was problematical and whose contents known to few.

In the intervals between circuits he went about egging people on to make music, and being asked to come and lecture again. His gods were Mendelssohn and Schumann; and it is as well to have gods, even if they are not immortal, or if you believe in them on the whole for the wrong reasons—Mendelssohn less for his scherzos and orchestration than for his neat tunes, and Schumann for his symphonies and chamber music rather than his early songs. He was of his own age; and perhaps our superior taste is only a change of fashion. He would probably have agreed with George Watts—"Don't ask me to criticize pictures: I always like them." He records, without endorsing, his friend William Johnson's (Cory's) view: "I feel that Handel's music is 'borné', like the talk of Parliamentary men and port-wine men, like the heroic couplets of Dryden and Dr. Johnson, whereas Mozart . . ." And when S. S. Wesley essays to quench his enthusiasm for the Hallelujah Chorus, he dockets him as "an organist who is much given to paradox and a general mover of amendments to any form of expressed opinion"; although, a few pages on, he fears "the incessant formalism of Handel will be a trouble to me for this short remainder of my days" (thirty-three years, in point of fact—he died just before the war).

There is an example of the cultivated amateur, a product that has never been rare in our country, and that has done much good in and to whatever walk of life it entered. One asks oneself what exactly it has contributed; and the first answer that occurs is taste. But "taste" is too much bound up with idiosyncrasy, and is no real answer, because there is no disputing about tastes. It would be better to say "reverence"—not blind reverence for authority, but open-eyed reverence for whatever ought to be revered, a belief in a standard, and a determination not to lower it or see it lowered. The type used to pass through Eton and King's, Winchester and New College, and other combinations; but the world is wider now, and the essential part of culture is to be found in many places. That essential is that a man should know how to learn, should know when he knows and when he does not; and it is an advantage that he should acquire this knowledge over something that will *not* be directly useful to him in after-life, because there is then some hope that he will come to his life-work with a resilient mind, and a spirit that has sloughed off the parochial and the poke-a-moke.

Over against the upholders of this general education stand those who believe in early specialization. Their view finds various vent: "If only I had not wasted so much time on the classics!"; "there is time for everything at the Royal College except music"; "the amateurishness of music teaching in this country"; "wealthy dilettantes"; "the right of way from chorister to cathedral organist is now closed"; and a heap more. Behind the impatient exaggeration of all these lurks one simple truth—that the English refuse to professionalize music, or anything else. We invented most of the outdoor games. They are the one form of art we wholly believe in, and we are correspondingly distressed when the Olympic competitors begin to reduce them to a science. The Romans regarded music as a mere adornment of life; to us it is an indoor game, to be played with its attendant risks from scant rehearsals. A foreign orchestra comes here, and we say the plain truth about its playing— that it is better than anything we can do; and add, under our breath—or want, really, to do. Opera seasons come and go; we wail over the absence of continuity and tradition, but we are never quite sure we could face the "alte Schlendrian" of the State-aided affair, any more than we could the dullness of the State-owned railway.

The crucial case arises with the Menuhins. They may be born in this country, but we do not often succeed in breeding them. The last case was probably that of Master Aspull, whom Rossini pronounced "the most extraordinary creature in Europe". How would you train a Menuhin? The advice to give him a wise father, as Menuhin has, is good; but it usually comes too late, and the plan of the rising generation to train their parents, so that they should not make any more mistakes, has hardly as yet gone beyond the experimental stage. The plan with us is to make the abnormal boy into a man, first by giving him a normal education (so that he doesn't die of consumption like George Aspull, at nineteen, or of early starvation like Schubert, at thirty-one, or of nerves racked in youth like Mozart, at thirty-five), and a musician afterwards. We hope that his musicality will survive it, but it usually doesn't. Then come the wiseacres, who blame it all on to the public

school "system", forgetting that the English could
have made quite different schools if they had been so
minded—but they weren't. They may be quite wrong,
but they decided to cover the ground with a carpet of
snow and let the crocuses push up through that if they
could. They therefore produced a nation of amateurs.
We had better make the best of them.

THE B.B.C. AND ITS CRITICS

(OCTOBER 1930)

A HEAVENLY body has swum into ken, displacing the
ether. Stars are rushing from their courses. Until
the music of the spheres can readjust itself to the new
conditions, the harmonious atmosphere of this poor
earth must remain charged with thunderbolt and levin.
Signals of distress are being sent up from many quarters.
The Birmingham festival is, for the present, no more.
Norwich is wondering how it will face another year.
Manchester is counting losses and trying to calm its
fears. The staid old Philharmonic that has weathered
so many storms is navigating warily. Nobody is quite
happy. Ἔρρει τὰ καλά.

But need anybody be quite unhappy? Music is a thing
of the spirit, untouched by physical developments; it
merely absorbs them, as daily life absorbs such things
as the disappearance of the horse, our servant for a whole
millennium, or the incidence of an earth-shaking war.
The majority, who do not make music, suppose it to be

contained in concerts, as, if they do not paint or write, they suppose painting to be in galleries and poetry in books. But a nation that is poet, painter, or musician lives those things. It sees the unseen in the seen: it hears the unheard in the heard. The musical moment reduces chaotic sound to order, turns prose into poetry. It lies on the edge of things—the little more and the little less. It may come from a vast undertaking involving a hundred players: it may come from a girl singing in the garden because it is a fine day; it has nothing to do with size, but a great deal to do with sincerity. The talk about high-brow and low-brow, too, is beside the mark: we are all both, but over different things. Anyone who really means what he says, and lives it, is absolved from both charges.

The people who hold this possession in fee simple are rarer than flattery would lead us to think; but we all must have some leasehold, or at least usufruct, of it, or we should not be able to recognize them. And that slight tenure is held at the cost of our criticism, which we exercise by our right to vote, or withhold the vote, in our public applause, or in switching on or off in private. For if we say that time is the true critic, how do we suppose that time works except through an audience of few or many? But concerts have uses beyond that of training the audiences of the future. They tell the composers to get busy and the executant to keep on practising: they provide objective and focus for the work of both. There must be bad concerts, as there must be weeds in a garden; but the better the concert, the stronger the incentive to make music throughout the country. When concerts drop off the audience is temporarily disappointed, but the harm done to the cause of music appears later. The instigators of concerts have in the past been the Church, the opera, and private patrons, but for different reasons the permanent inducements offered by those bodies no longer exist. A new body if it appeared would be a godsend.

> Hark, hear you not a heavenly harmony?
> Is't Jove, think you, that plays upon the spheres?

The B.B.C. is permanent, since it is in tune with the age; it is beneficent, for it brings gifts; and it is a powerful patron because it is not private, but public. It is true it is not musical by profession, for patrons are not as a rule that. It does not even play the flute, like Frederick the Great—which is perhaps a mercy, for then our composers would have to write down to its amateur capacities, as Quantz and others did, and our theorists to compose a "Method". It simply performs the whole duty of a patron, to pay the flautist and call the tune. And it is over that that the trouble has arisen, for it has made so bold as to choose its own flautist, or rather its hautboy player. That matters much, because good hautboys, once so common, are now precious possessions, and a good horn is worth his weight in gold. No one knows how far the bandits of Savoy, as they are called, mean to go, and people are asking what is the ethics of it all.

Before we discuss that, let us assure Sir Hamilton Harty, who feels himself aggrieved, of our sympathy. His energies have made his orchestra into a noble instrument; our ears tell us that every time we hear them under him. There is no orchestra here that consistently plays with more force and accuracy, and none that is so conspicuous for its *esprit de corps*. Though he said it himself, it is none the less true that his men can compete with the foreign orchestras; and he put his finger on the reason when he said that an orchestra learns best under one man. He must feel now, at the beginning of a season, as a colonel does when H.Q. commandeers his adjutant just as his regiment is going on service. He made that player what he is, and others are to profit by it. When he tells us that wireless provides music "with the bloom off it" he will find more agreement than when he questions the cultural value of its efforts, or describes its "penny plain and twopence coloured" (from the studio or the concert room) as "doing evil that good may come", or asks pettishly if "the North is to pay for the South *and* be raided of its players". His feelings have here run away with his judgment a little.

Hear the other side. Wireless presentation of an orchestra is as yet far from perfect. A simple proof of this is that unless you know beforehand who is conducting you are not likely to guess from what you hear. But in the first place, those who cannot reach concerts will not lose much from this fact. In the second, the deaf and the blind (both in the letter and in the spirit) are brought back in a wonderful way to our common life, and they are too overjoyed at this boon to ask for minutiae. Thirdly, even thorough-paced musicians find it useful; they get the structure as a whole, the tempo, the time it takes to perform, and, with a score before them, much of the detail, except in the *tuttis*; also many hints about phrasing and reading, and some guidance as to what of the new music is thought worth doing. All this

cannot be described as of little value; and if Sir Thomas
Beecham and Sir Hamilton Harty exhaust their vocabulary upon the debasement of their ideal, it is only what
they ought to do, and what we, who have the vaguest
idea of what orchestral music might be until they show
us, ought not.

But the direct issue that Sir Hamilton Harty raises is
the ethics of "raiding". Surely the free disposal of one's
services is the best system, all round, in a free country.
If a man could not be allowed to better himself, however
valuable, neither ought he to be liable to dismissal,
however useless, and there comes a time when the
trumpet's lips go and the violin's bow-hand trembles.
The raidee must decide, and one way or another it will
not always mean his going. But even if it generally did,
and the B.B.C. were gradually to absorb all the best
players in the country, and if they were eventually to
multiply—supposing their cash and the crowded state
of the ether permitted it—their present 114 players
by two or even three, so as to play all kinds of music,
day and night, to anyone in any part of the British Isles,
would it do any harm to music?

Certainly not; it would probably do much good. The
higher the peaks, the greater the area of the mountain
range. If they are going to offer a prize for the best men,
more men will try to become best. On the other hand,
money will not do everything, and it has a pernicious
habit of making people ask for more. It will be something
to have got rid of deputies, but a much harder task
remains—to implant and foster a spirit of loyalty and
esprit de corps. It is easy to be loyal to a man, difficult
to be loyal to a corporation. The corporation will prob-

ably find it necessary to import not only the best players, but also the best conductors, and to give to each a unit of his own which he may be proud of leading.

The B.B.C. has done wonders in its short six years —to speak here, as is proper, only of its music. Of course, we grouse a good deal or we should not be Englishmen; but to have bred such a race of critics is in itself an achievement, for there was a time when these same people knew nothing of music and cared less.

APPRAISAL AND CRITICISM

LET us look at some of the actual facts of a life which might be symbolized in a poem, a poem that music could in its turn symbolize.

At a certain time in a certain place the terminal reports came to be written, and in order to economize space (and imagination) comment was confined in these to the letters G, F, M, and B. And there was a certain Irish boy who had never managed throughout the term to bring simultaneously to any lesson his book, his pen, his wits, and his attention; though he sometimes brought other things, such as a little jam at the corner of the mouth, or a smell of burning, or, on saints' days perhaps, a tame snake. His form master wore a white tie, and if he had been living three hundred and seventy-eight years ago he would no doubt have sent Latimer to the stake, or with equal heart have gone there himself. When he came to O'Brien's report, he wrote in red ink a bold

"B." with a definite full stop. When the reports were sorted out and sent to the housemasters, Burke, an Irishman, with his fatal facility for seeing both sides of any question, dipped his pen in green ink and wrote "Not so terribly B."; and beneath that again the Head wrote in his legibly-illegible hand: "I hope he will come back to earn his housemaster's report." Term followed term, and eventually O'Brien, who could not accomplish Sandhurst, was pushed somehow into a Goorkha regiment. Neither his captain nor anyone else called him a credit to it on parade, but in three months he had nicknamed the whole mess, and in six he had shown his men how to win two matches. Some years later, when their troopship, rotten with dysentery, was hanging about off Mespot, it was he who kept despair at bay. When they shivered on the western front, he borrowed and stole blankets for them. When they went in with their kukris at Loos, he did not come back. On the spot where he was last seen a schoolfellow put up a piece of wood with his name, and after it (mentally) a "G".

We saw that three appraisals were given of the conduct of O'Brien: one praised, another blamed—and both of these are hard to bear, the one by the modest the other by the vain—and the third was negative. We all pass such judgments every day and have them passed upon us. Praise is usually called "appreciation" and blame "criticism", and both wrongly. In an appraisal a performance is put in at one end of the machine and praise or blame comes out at the other. But true criticism is the salt of life. It is not deep thinking or bold action but tense imagination. When a man has it, it is not a playing fast and loose with facts, not a nimble use of

M

metaphor, not a mere inquisitiveness; it is the seeing eye, the hearing ear,

> His very serviceable suit of black
> Was comely once and conscientious still,
> And many might have worn it, though none did.
>
> He glanced o'er books on stalls with half an eye,
> And fly-leaf ballads on the vendor's string,
> And broad-edged bold-print posters on the wall
> He took such cognizance of men and things,
> If any beat a horse, you felt he saw,
> If any cursed a woman, he took note;
> Yet stared at nobody—you stared at him,
> And found, less to your pleasure than surprise,
> He seemed to know you and expect as much.
>
>   Bless us, all the while,
> How sprucely we are dressed out, you and I;
> A second, and the angels alter that.

A CRITIC'S PROBLEMS

THEIR POSSIBLE SOLUTION

COULD we for a moment put aside all the irrelevant and sometimes unworthy views held about it, and examine dispassionately the critic's job? Assuming that the first requirements have been met—that the world has been told of what is happening in music (or being written, or disputed about, or going to happen), that the right bouquets have been handed to or withheld from the right people, that there has been no leakage as between the fountain pen and the font, and that the opinion as delivered is free from errors of fact, of expression, and of printing—what is it, ultimately, that words can hope to say about tones?

Tones have been before now, and we always hope they may be again, among the most moving experiences of a lifetime. We approach new tones as the angler approaches the backwash below the weir, well knowing that by the time he gets there the fly may be off the water, but agog with the glorious uncertainty of the time and the place and the right man meeting. When tones do move us, they move us so deeply that words about them seem a sort of profanation; that they are written about at all is in itself a kind of admission that they are not really felt, for if they had been felt the only natural reply would have been silence, as Mark Twain eloquently hinted of the Alpine sunrise.

Three things have lately moved those who heard them, and have provoked chatter among those who did not. In Toscanini's conduct of the B.B.C. concerts we had an edition-de-luxe of works we know well, and felt what it is that eloquence adds to style, the ideal fusion of discrepant elements—counterpoint, rhythm and timbre, or, as we might say, thought, will and feeling—and we came out elated. At Glyndebourne we heard every artistic force bent to one purpose, the doing justice to Mozart's opera. And why? Just because a man got the maggot in his brain that, if you believe in a thing, nothing is too much to sacrifice for perfection. And this was an Englishman: mad, therefore; but it was moving. And

on May 24, 1935, we met to try to say to the King and
Queen what words cannot say, and we used music to do
it. And there we, all unconsciously, gave the lie to our
own nature and said, unashamed, well-knowing what we
admitted, and not caring, that music moves us as deeply
as any game. These are the things the critic hopes may
somehow leak out from his queer medley of jargon,
anecdote and metaphor.

TERMINOLOGY

EACH art has its special terminology—specific, "soffit",
"tempera", "enjambment", "arpeggio"; or general,
"order", "perspective", "scansion", "key". The specific
terms give little trouble; we can guess half of them
(except in architecture) and look up the rest. But the
general words there is no getting at short of considerable
familiarity with, and some thinking about, the particular
art. An architect would probably be sorry to have to
define the ionic "order" so that a tiro would never
make a mistake over a given instance. A painter, who
described "perspective", though truly enough, as the
art of making things look lifelike on a plane surface,
would feel that he had left a good deal unsaid, yet if he
said more he would have to become technical. "Scansion"
is a slippery thing; if you measure it, you are probably
wrong, if you feel it, you are probably right. A "key"
should lock or unlock something; it doesn't, and so must
have a paragraph of its own.

Let us start with half a paragraph from Mr. H. W. Fowler's *If Wishes Were Horses* (Allen and Unwin):—

At an Oxford bump-supper, as someone sat down after singing *John Peel*, my neighbour observed to me that he had done it in (if I remember) four different keys. I had been quite satisfied, and was much distressed by the criticism, not because I was concerned for the singer's credit, but because of this horrible reinforcement to my conscious deficiencies. Ever since, I have recognized that music is a sealed book, and have taken the greatest care to ascertain that no-one is within earshot when I allow my high or my low spirits to express themselves vocally; they very likely do so in a dozen keys at once.

And to this follows a terrible confession. *I was that neighbour.* If I had known *my* neighbour's feelings, and if I had thought about the matter more than one and twenty has had time to think, I should have added that a different key for each verse was better in place under the circumstances than one key for all. For to "lose one's key" is entirely analogous to a bonfire in the quad., to waking the echoes of eight centuries with an Australian stock-whip, and other abrogations of logic. The judge who summed up, "Prisoner at the bar, God gave you health and strength, instead of which you go about stealing cows" temporarily lost his key; he forgot what his first clause had said when he framed his second. Mr. Fowler, and many others, would see this easily in language, which they have spoken, read and written all their lives; they only do not see it in music because it has not come their way to sing or play, read, or write it. We *hear* music; and if you wish to know what language is like when you only hear it, consider a memsahib's knowledge of Hindustani, or an Orient Express courier's knowledge of English—and, shall we add, the switcher-on's knowledge of music who sings *The Rosary*, who can't read a score, and who writes to the B.B.C. to say they are rotten or, far worse, rather decent.

The present writer has received from time to time exhortation to write what the ordinary man can understand. But who is the ordinary man? Let us turn again to Mr. Fowler:

> It is not possible for any man, unless he is only recording concrete facts, to be really frank with a miscellaneous audience; he may intend to be understood as much as he will; but he speaks a dialect, and his dialect will be misinterpreted by all but a few who happen to speak the same; the brain has dialects as well as the tongue, and no man can speak the same as everyone else, because the equals of unequals are unequal.

Meanwhile, the man he has tried to write for may be shortly described. This man, a particular man who could be named, knows and cares what goes on in the world of music. He estimates quickly and justly. He remembers tunes. He does not forget impressions. He can play half "the 48", and accompany songs not harder that Schubert or Parry. He cannot read a full score. He has not written music, or else he has written and said nothing. He chooses what he will hear, and it may include Monteverde or Stravinsky; in either case he can rely on a horse-sense. He has no prejudice for or against the British composer; he contents himself with putting a job in a British executant's way when he can, just to see how he shapes. His comments are usually kind, but can be quite severe.

"HACKNEYED"

THE *Oxford Dictionary* distinguishes "trite" as "commonplace, worn out", and "hackneyed" as "made trite, or made common". A *trite* quotation, for instance, is one which the average mind inevitably makes in a given contingency, such as *"Naturam expellas furca"* (hoping perhaps to make it less trite by *not* going on *"tamen usque recurret"*): the man is using it exactly as Horace meant it, and the only objection is that many, too many, people have done so before him; to which he retorts *"Pereant qui ante nos nostra"*. The competition for the most *hackneyed* quotation in the English language would probably be severe; high up in it would certainly come "a thing of beauty is a joy for ever". As to this line the world may be divided into several classes: (1) those who know who wrote it, and those who don't; (2) those who knowing that, are not sure whether it begins *Hyperion* or *Endymion*; (3) those who, knowing that, have or have not read the poem, so as to know how Keats understood beauty; and (4) those who can or those who cannot go on with it—

> Its loveliness increases; it will never
> Pass into nothingness; but still will keep
> A bower quiet for us, and a sleep
> Full of sweet dreams, and health, and quiet breathing.

—and so become aware that this is the most powerful indictment of hackneydom there can be. There is a kind of man who will let fall that line over a well-coloured meerschaum, a kind of woman who will murmur it when a basket of fruit appears at dessert; and then remembering, he that he may drop his pipe the next minute in the fender, she that fruit is there to be eaten, they wonder why the poet said "for ever"; whereas if they had read and attended to him they would have seen that he means not unending time but only felt, deep-seated, uttermost quality—much as the Bible speaks of "eternal" life, or Matthew Arnold of the nightingale's "eternal" pain.

Single lines of Shakespeare and single verses of the Bible undoubtedly are hackneyed in this way; whole psalms are to an organist, and possibly 1 Cor. xv. is to an undertaker. They have been performed for him too often by people who either did not feel much, or into whose feelings he could not enter. And it is performance, too, by which music is "made common, or trite"; the music itself is always potentially fragrant. Unfortunately, it is the best music that is most hackneyed because that is hardest for players to rise to the full meaning of. A writer in the *Manchester Guardian* said lately that the *Fifth Symphony* "is not hackneyed in Manchester". One can well believe it; the Halle Orchestra are not likely to reduce anything they play to that state; but in London it is possibly both more hackneyed and better played. The *Chaconne* is the sort of thing that becomes a *pons asinorum*; so is the *Appassionata*. Nicholas Rubenstein was to play something for two pianos, and his partner had to be given an audition; "Tell her to play the *Appassionata*", he petulantly called out from the next room, where he was dressing.

The man who knows how to put his soul into a thing

is not common. I came across him once; he used to read philosophy for Greats for an hour, and be afterwards as white as a sheet; if the first six scholars of England were now named he would be among them. Music is possibly harder than philosophy, because, besides the brain, it engages the nerves. It is neither of those that is lacking in this island; it is faith. For the great majority music is an amenity, to be switched on after the home covert has been shot or the crossword solved. No harm in that; what matters is what the believers believe. "He is passionately fond of music". Is he? What does he do with it, or for it? Will he forgo leisure, forget his meals, face poverty? Will the blood all leave his face after he has spent an hour on the *Appassionata*? Until that minority appears—never mind the majority—music will continue to be spoken of, occasionally, as "hackneyed".

MUSICAL PSYCHOLOGY

HAS anyone yet overheard Mr. Harold Samuel, who fingers according to a law of his own, or Sir Thomas Beecham, whose wit is equal to any musical conundrum that is presented to it, or Sir Edward Elgar, who takes what sounds he wants from the circumambient air, talking about the way in which they "perceive" or "apprehend" or "cognize" music? "You weigh the stars", says Mephistopheles,

> You weigh the stars, and split the atom,
> Only to let them be, when all is ended,
> As God intended.

TECHNIQUE

IMITATION

L ISTENING to *Siegfried* lately one thought about these
imitations of natural sounds. Are they music? Was
music born in the swayings of reeds and the voice of
the wind as Lucretius thought? As our orchestral
mechanism is gradually perfected, do we get any nearer
the voice of Nature; and is that what we are actually
aiming at?

O Blackbird, what a boy you are,
　　How you do go it!
Blowing your bugle to that one sweet star—
　　How you do blow it!

Yes, it must be blackbird. How he practises all the
spring, hammering away at one phrase till he gets it to
his liking, getting cross with himself when it won't come
right, and then—here it is, the finished product, sealing
the fate of his lady and reducing all rivals to despair!

But Wagner said "Waldvogel"; not any particular bird, but birdiness in general; whereas Beethoven in the *Sixth* said definitely, "nightingale, quail and cuckoo", besides giving them the conventional trill and dactyl and pyrrhic that we all know. What did these composers mean, each of them? Was it this? Wagner said, "Yes, of course, you are in a wood, and my bird-voice will show you that far more clearly than the stage-manager's gauze trees and gold and silver spot-lights; but I shouldn't have dragged it in unless it was going to be a personage in the drama, and to talk a good deal of sense." And Beethoven: "You see, these birds' voices are nothing to me in themselves; I've written my whole movement without using any one of them as a theme. If my music is any good, it has placed you there already without them; I only put them in to remind you that art does not go so deep as Nature, nor Nature soar so high as art."

"Frogs!" said Handel; "frogs 'in thy bedchamber and upon thy bed, into thine ovens and into thy kneading-troughs.' Let us have frogginess, then; but why should we waste it? Tunes are hard enough to come by, anyhow; why, I have to borrow a good many of mine, and there are some ill-conditioned people who call it stealing —the sort of barefaced thing that Buononcini did. Frogs, indeed! By the time I've done with them, there won't be much doubt about the facts of the matter. Besides, why does *der liebe Gott* make things happen at all if they are not to be put into my music; works of man and works of Nature, they are all for His glory, and so is my music. It is true, I shall have to keep on jumping when it comes to the 'blotches and blains', which are placid and persistent enough; but that is Dr. Bentley's fault."

So there are at least three reasons for imitating Nature: Wagner wanted to create illusion, Beethoven to point a moral, and Handel to get on with his job. And all three of them, when it came to the point, were forced down to a particular instance; for imitation "in a general way" does not amount to much. *Waldweben* is a beautiful piece of imagination, but the "murmurs" of the forest are not half so real as they were in *Siegfried*; at most they remind us of something we once knew. The *Battle of Vittoria*, on the other hand, is unimaginative, but the quotations of French and English trumpet calls still do not manage, for all their similitude, to induce reality. Mere imitation is not enough, then: to be any good it must say something beyond itself and clinch what the music is already saying; and to do that, it cannot be too lifelike. No doubt orchestral resources are greater in each successive generation: Strauss's sheep are more lifelike than Purcell's turtledoves. But the danger now is that we shall have too many Mossolov factories and Honegger 231's without enough musical content. Orchestras create these things as armies create wars.

But to go back to our question—*was* music born of winds and streams and reeds, or even of birds and beasts, who perhaps have the first stirrings of an artistic consciousness? We may agree with Lucretius V. 1376 that imitating bird calls and noticing the sound of the wind blowing through the interstices of the reeds came long before the making of songs and of pipes with holes. But we shall probably think that man had a far more imperious desire in himself. Music to him meant magic and medicine and power over others, and as long as it cast spells, or healed, or bent friend or foe to his will,

he had a motive that transcended any artistic pleasure.
The essence of the spell lay in its exactitude; if it varied
by a demisemiquaver, the god would not be appeased
nor the patient cured. Accuracy is a good beginning for
any art, but the dead hand is fatal in music as in speech.
His use of tones was as strictly utilitarian as the birds;
but it was not till he could put himself outside that, and
reflect, as (one supposes) a bird cannot, that he could
make music worth the name: and then he only liked it
"after he had well eaten and drunk, when everybody
is prepared to like anything"—the old "social amenity"
view, in fact (the Roman and the English), amply suffi-
cient, if one believed in it, to account for their being the
two least musical nations on earth. But one does not quite
believe in it, for reasons that may be given some other day.

IN TUNE

SYRINX! What a pretty name! The grasshopper's
cry on a sweltering summer morning is in it. It was
the name of the lady Pan loved, and when he tried to kiss
her, and she eluded him, and he clutched a handful of
reeds on the river bank instead, and lay panting, the
wind got up in the reeds with a sound like lamentation,
and he, touched by the sweetness of the music, made the
Pipes of Pan in memory of her. "Grove" knows nothing
of all this; he has only a thing he calls "the Pandean
pipes" (nobody knows where he got that "d" from),
reminding us of "pandemonium" and "pandering" and

"pandects" and all sorts of horrors. The lady's name has been used for pure irrelevancies like a "subterranean cavern", an "elephant's trunk", and the "Eustachian tube" but also for something much worthier—the instrument on which the lark plays in the morning and the nightingale in the evening; but the memorial of her has covered half the earth, and she is the mother of all them that handle the pipe and organ.

For when a boy blows down a key he takes out of his pocket, and then down a "squeaker" he cuts from the hazel in May, he is doing, separately, two things that differ only in size and arrangement from what the man who plays the Hallelujah chorus at the Albert Hall does together. If he puts several squeakers in a row he has a mouth organ, and if several hollow keys of different lengths, he has a syrinx, though he would soon make a handier syrinx with different lengths of gas-piping. Having made the latter he is confronted with the question, *how* different the lengths should be; in other words, what scale he shall adopt. If he is an English boy of to-day it is settled for him by centuries of convention. We wanted to have harmony *and*—this is the crux—the power of modulating at any moment to some other key, *and this* on a keyboard instrument which has fixed tones. The three intervals, which make the whole of our harmony, move in different planes; m octaves never make n fifths, p fifths never make q major thirds: and so we have to take a little off the fifth and put a good deal on to the third to make them fit with the octave. Our tuners spend a couple of years learning how to put their keyboard out of tune by the right amount, and you can see and hear the result on the pianoforte, namely, that three thirds do make an octave, and that twelve fifths do make seven octaves, and you will not notice the very small out-of-tuneness. That is the last stage in a long history that has made the present convention (and there are various plans for the future): and in that convention a scale is implied which we all know.

We talk of a fifth as if it were a real thing: but it is an abstraction. The fifth that legend tells us Pythagoras got by weights (a hammer on different anvils) was one thing; a plucked or bowed fifth is another; a blown fifth another. When you blow down a C pipe, for instance, and try to get the G above it by overblowing, it comes out, strange to say, very flat—a quarter of the way, in fact, to F sharp. So now suppose the boy, instead of being English, is the only musical member of an aboriginal family on a desert island where there are plenty of bamboos. He does not want harmony, only melody; so he does not require thirds. He builds his scale therefore with fifths, as we once did—F—C—G—D—A—E—B (= CDEFGAB). Six fifths, there are; and each of them a quarter of a semitone flat, so that his B will be to our ears three-quarters of a tone flat on his F. But not to his ears. He got his interval from Nature, just as we do ours; and all that has happened is that she told *him* one thing because he was using only bamboos, and only in a particular way, and *us* another because we have used every conceivable material in every conceivable way. It is as difficult for us to think that his melody is in tune as to believe that the sun goes round the earth; he believes it is the sun that moves, not the earth, and knows that his melody is in tune.

Now expand the desert island into that large part of

the earth's surface which we call China, Java, a good many
of the Pacific islands, Peru and probably other States of
South America, and you have the region that started at
least, and to some extent has continued, on this peculiar
system of music, as a basis. No doubt some of them have
gone much further, and have even, though by a different
route, come to make what we, in our ignorance, call
music; but the "shame of the swaddling clothes" is on
them all, and their music to us, as ours to them, must
remain a sealed book. We may ask, therefore, why we
should trouble ourselves about such matters at all. One
reason is that they provide a clear picture of what it is
to be in tune or out of tune. For people not seldom
ask "What do you mean by 'being in tune'? What is
in tune with what?" And the answer, that "the interval
sung or played is in tune with what Nature provides",
is best understood by considering what she provided
elsewhere, by seeing how long it took us to arrive at
her true meaning, and by realizing why we were right to
falsify it.

And another reason for going into these matters is
that there is no precision in music till instruments bring
it. We all know that the voice without instruments
(if there ever was such a state of things) sings in the five-
note scale, and that the two more which make our seven-
note scale came by way of instruments, and very variously,
since instruments are very various. But he would be a
rash man who should say he knew how that five-note
scale was tuned, because it, almost certainly, varied
slightly with each singer; whereas it couldn't vary
on an instrument without our knowing it. For instance,
the Hindus have twenty-two quarter-tones in the

octave—a funny number, because the octave has six tones, and four times six . . . etc. I once spent a year out there, trying to make out what had happened, without success. But I brought home a bundle of facts; and now a certain Dr. Lachmann has argued from them to the instrument on which they must have been played originally; and this turns out to be a Chinese *K'in*. If you are interested in these movements of the dim past which have moulded the present, and can read German, may I suggest to your notice the *Gesellschaft zur Erforschung der Musik des Orients* (Sec. Johannes Wolf, Unter den Linden 36, Berlin)? Further, to any energetic young man with the requisite knowledge, that he should get leave to translate the books of Erich v. Hornbostel and Robert Lachmann which are entirely unknown here? And lastly, that we ought to wake up about the science of musicology (—we haven't even got the word, you see). The Continent is far ahead of us in many respects. There are plenty of other things we know about, but in this matter we are like Henri Quatre, who, when asked if he could play the violin, answered, "I never tried it."

CONTENT AND FORM

ON a certain occasion lately Dr. Vaughan Williams "thought aloud" for a quarter of an hour, and then sat down under the hallucination that he was boring his audience with a lecture. That was regrettable: for if he who has been through it all does not tell us, how

N

should we know? However, what he did say was the truth: *there is no music except what people make*—make with their own voices or fingers or pens. The interesting point was, he said, what the young were making. What were they thinking? Were they expressing what they truly thought? Were they going down into their real selves? Yes: the universities seemed to be doing so. They were helping to create the atmosphere in which the real man might be born and would grow. Bach, the man of men, could never have done what he did unless he had breathed such an atmosphere. And there were others: music is thought more of, it is thought of as a thing worth intelligent study. That was not so once.

We should have liked to know how to translate this into act. And yet, is it not better we should make our own translation? "There is no music except what people make." Well then, everybody is in the right who plugs away at his own little corner of it; who goes on playing the fiddle badly only because he can't yet play it well, who shreds in a useful bass in a choir only because he wants to get deeper inside the man's thoughts, who writes and burns and writes again only that he may come to understand Bach better, who goes to a college of music not to learn how to get a living, but only how "by patience to find his own soul". "We are a nation of amateurs, and thank God for it", said Vaughan Williams—and there stopped. May we continue? There are those who fancy that the Greeks, from the high place they gave to "musiké", put music as such on a higher pedestal in their thoughts than we do. Nothing of the kind. They did not care two straws about Dorian and Phrygian in themselves. Their interest was partly mythological—and you must allow a nation its ontological framework; and partly ethical—they asked, with Dryden: "What passions cannot music raise and quell?" Well, they were amateurs. They valued music (and painting and poetry and sculpture and architecture) for what they could contribute to the making of the whole man. And were they wrong?

One thing Dr. Vaughan Williams said was of interest to those who wrestle with the music put forth to-day. He confessed that he had been unable to make out what it was trying to express, what attitude of mind or what conviction was behind it. He was speaking to a coterie of literary people and therefore keeping his words quite general; but we understood that it was not "the idiom" that was the puzzle, but the underlying purpose—what are sometimes called its "spiritual values". For if one cannot believe of music that it comes from the centre of a man's being, and that that being has a purpose tenaciously held, no technical ingenuities will keep it alive. There is nothing puritanic about this. The "purpose" may quite as well be merry as serious; the only condition is that it should be heartwhole. He is writing his third opera; it is of the merry kind. We shall probably find, whether it attracts or repels us personally, that the merriment is given deep anchorage in the music, as adventure was in the "sea symphony" and adoration in *Job*. Music can tell us no details: even the line that marks off merry from serious is by no means clear cut. It ought to tell us the size of the man's mind and heart, and then it has done its duty.

That is on the whole a conception of the content of music. Professor Dent, the active President of the

Musical Association, addressed himself about the same time to its form. He was by no means thinking aloud, but reading a carefully written paper on "the Romantic spirit in music". He did not define "romantic". He said we all knew what was meant. We do not, of course: but if he puts it on that ground we shall have to say that we suppose "romantic" and "classic" are terms that art adopts because it declines to soil its fingers with such mundanities as "liberal" and "conservative". He examined Weber, as typical of the time when the Liberals had a particularly long innings, and found that he had two levers of progress—the appoggiatura and dotted rhythm (a form of accacciatura). He dated the first of these from the seventeenth century, which was astonishing, considering that folksong is full of it. He defined form as "placing the effective moments where they will best tell". This seemed particularly happy. It embraces the composer's favourite dictum, that "each work of art has its own form", it supports the commonly held belief that the real *diabolus in musica* is anticlimax, and it falls in with the convictions of literature.

Professor Dent was concerned only with "the swing of the pendulum". He assumed conservative and liberal conventions, and took stock only of the steps by which the latter leaven the former. That is not the position to-day. There are no conventions. There is red revolution. Brahms was the last die-hard. He tried to patch up a peace between the Klopstocks and Herders and the Shelleys and Byrons of music. But after Wagner there was no peace: hence, incidentally, the famous manifesto. Brahms—his music, that is—went into retreat. If it is now emerging again, that is because we are sick of revolution and sigh for something stable. There must be conventions—rules; for art is "knowing how to break rules": no art is possible while the principles of the constitution are being violated every day. Polyphony has no meaning when it is huddled up in vertical harmony; rhythm none, when it is a mere idle spectator of the achievements of harmony; harmony none, when stripped of the significance rhythm would have given; new scales none, when there is no accepted scale from which they can be felt as divergences.

We ail then here, and here. We write music that lacks content, because we will not take the trouble to mean all that we might. We might be ourselves, and we prefer to be somebody else; or we choose superficial aspects of thoughts and things, when we might be our real selves. The remedy is in our own hands: we can make more music instead of buying it. The Vic-Wells has set us an example: is that going to stand alone? And we write music that lacks form, because we have got rid of all our artistic beliefs, we challenge everything, we do not hold that there are any fundamentals that should not be touched. The remedy has not yet been seen; we are battling it out. It may come of what is known as "neoclassicism", an ill-defined attempt to reinstate the old classical balances in terms of the new harmony. That will either die out, like so many other "isms", or will define itself better. The great man, when he comes, will decide: we must hope he is not so far off as 1985, where Dr. Vaughan Williams put him.

TEMPO RUBATO

THIS is a thing we all of us do every day, though we have no name for it. It is the act of dwelling on or skimming. If we could phonograph on the spot a public speaker, or an ordinary conversation, or ourselves when we read a letter aloud in order to get at its sense quickly, we should find hurryings and delays. We should also find it very hard to say where those hurries or delays exactly began and ended, or to show in any way, except by actually executing them, how they were to be done. No two readers or speakers will make them exactly alike, nor is there the least need that they should do so. The English language is the servant of all of us, and the quality of the service depends entirely on the way in which the servant is used.

Thus, in these lines of Milton,

> But listen not to his temptations; warn
> Thy weaker; let it profit thee to have heard,
> By terrible example, the reward
> Of disobedience; firm they might have stood,
> Yet fell; remember, and fear to transgress.

after we have minded our stops—which music would have represented by longer notes or by rests (silences) —and have made an infinitesimal pause at the end of the line—to mark the versification—and have heightened the accentuation of the salient words a little—because they are weighty and because it is poetry, we shall all agree that the second line moves faster than the fifth, and that there is no need for all the five to move at the same pace;

though we should not be prepared to lay down the law for other readers as to what the pace should be, or even for ourselves, because we might feel differently about it next Tuesday.

From some correspondence lately received it would seem that this irregularity within regularity is a difficult matter to grasp. But it ought not to be. It is all around us every day. The quickened step, the flushed cheek, the impatient hands, and, again, other movements which mark a provoking or humorous or ironical deliberation, are the tacit criticisms we all make on the monotone of life. Life has a certain average rhythm of its own, and we break it for a variety of reasons, at one end of which is an unaccountable inspiration and at the other pure cussedness. And the essence of the thing lies in the quality of the reason. When we feel, without knowing precisely why, that the reason is wrong, we describe the action (or speech, or behaviour) as fussy, or phlegmatic, or perhaps as merely picturesque. When we feel it, equally without analyzing, to be right, we say "how like him!" or, "he knows what he's doing", or "there's something big about him".

Music alone has a name for all this, because not only is manner to her all-important, but, owing to our own imperfections, we nearly always have to take all the music we get "in the manner of" somebody else. Instead of sitting in a proverbial armchair with our feet on a metaphorical fender and taking our music neat, we take it usually as a communal pleasure, fortified or diluted by the manner of a particular conductor or executant. Music calls this criticism of herself "tempo rubato", "robbed" time, as we talk of one organ stop robbing another (of wind), or the pedals robbing the Great (of a stop they don't possess). There is no idea whatever of paying back, any more than there was in the mind of MacHeath or Beau Brocade. And still less of paying back within the bar; that could be true only for those who think music in bars, and not, as they ought to, in pages. How this myth about paying back arose it would be difficult to say; perhaps some tender mind was shocked at the presence of immorality in a beautiful art. But art is as non-moral as Nature.

Another mistaken idea is that rubato can be the property or the speciality of any one man. A pamphlet has been written, perhaps more than one, on "Chopin's rubato". We might as well talk of Chopin's Bank rate, or Chopin's Equator. There is, indeed, a tradition that Chopin kept the left hand steadily on time while the right hand divagated. But this elementary idea was not peculiarly his own: it has been the common property of drummers (on a pair of drums, left and right) from immemorial time. What was peculiar to him was not this or that thing, but the way he fused them all, and there is no need to write about that because words will not say it, only the tones themselves. It is better, therefore, to remind people of what they have actually heard.

Donald Tovey comes, to any piece of music which he takes in hand, armed with a universal knowledge. He has considered all periods and styles, and followed out individual careers from early works to mature products. This knowledge, always on the simmer, bubbles over whenever he speaks or writes. He is so full and so assured of it that he can afford to play with it, and learning that might have been pedantic is witty. For him it is not enough that a passage might have this or that effective interpretation; the only interpretation that counts is that one which the man, judging from all that can be known of his work, must have meant. To arrive at this he has noted all relevant dates, compared one work with another, examined manuscripts, sketchbooks, letters, *obiter dicta*, everything that could bear on the point, and in every way lived himself into the man's life as it is displayed in his music. So when instead of speaking or writing his thoughts he plays them, we are dazzled by no flashes of brilliance; we warm our hands at the glow of a lifelong passion for truth.

Now when we hear such a man play, or others like him—for there have been others: Joachim was one and Richter was another, and the particular instrument they used makes little difference—we become aware, suddenly or gradually (that depends on ourselves), that he is taking our hand and telling us quickly what he has in his heart. He has pondered it all, and at length sees it all clearly, and is now telling us just as if he were talking; and even if we do not grasp the whole argument, we absolutely understand the tone of voice. Tap a finger to the time and watch it, and the eye is shocked at the astonishing liberties taken. Then stop tapping and only listen, and everything seems perfectly natural again. That is not "Tovey's rubato", but the true tempo rubato.

TEMPO

ORL.: There's no clock in the forest.
ROS.: Then there is no true lover in the forest.

"What a funny watch!" she remarked, "it tells the day
of the month, and doesn't tell what o'clock it is?"

"Why should it?" muttered the Hatter. "Does *your*
watch tell you what year it is?"

"Of course not," Alice replied very readily; "but
that's because it stays the same year for such a long time
together."

"Which is just the case with *mine*," said the Hatter.

HERE is irrefutable evidence from two unimpeachable
sources that time is relative, and that it is relative
to, or is measured by, what we can get into it—a season-
able thought for January 2nd. Certainly, as adventurous
Alice says, 1927 will stay the same year for such a long
time together, but equally certainly we hope it will not
go so slow as 1926, which is what the Hatter (whose only
notion of relieving boredom is to take a clean place, not
to do a new thing) means. And Orlando is so "love-
shaked" that one long day seems just like another, while
for Rosalind, time "trots hard", as for a young maid
between betrothal and wedding; "if the interim be but
a se'nnight, Time's pace is so hard that it seems the
length of seven year".

An hour, then, is not what it "is", but what it "seems".
What it is, is the seventy-two hundred ticks or so, *plus*
the fact that we count them, *plus* our recognition that the
clock hands have reached certain places on the dial.

But that is a large experience; and it is in relation to that that we call the hour long. If, on the other hand, we have attended not to a number of ticks, but to an interesting talk, we say, "How short the time has been: I can hardly believe it was a whole hour." The uninteresting ticks and the interesting talk both monopolize attention, but differently, and the "pace" of the hour depends not on the attention they ask in common, but on the interest in which they differ. But, again, we are just as likely to say after the talk, "What an age it seems; was it only an hour?" This seems to mean that we carry about with us an average expectation of the amount of interest that can normally be got into an hour, and that in the case of the talk the interest exceeded this; and the two sayings together show how entirely time is relative to what happens in it.

We carry this way of measuring time through life. We can say "the pace was furious" equally of a football match or of an argument, and we mean by it not that the legs in one case or the tongue in the other moved quicker, but that the events, physical or mental, followed each other with shorter gaps than usual between them. Painters will even talk of the tempo of a picture, where it is not motion, but the fact that fresh impressions succeed each other in space with less or more mediation between them. We feel a difference of pace between Froude and Macaulay, between Kipling and Stevenson. By a stretch of language we might similarly contrast a Gothic cathedral with a Greek temple.

But the contrast is more immediately felt in music than elsewhere, because every part of music is a time-relation—high or low pitch is a matter of quick or slow vibration, harmony and tone-colour are both questions of selecting pitches, and the third element is time proper. Melody, harmony and rhythm interpenetrate one another so completely that it is not easy to examine one of them in isolation. Jointly they make music, separately they make nothing; and theory, which can deal with only one thing at a time, mostly clutches the air. Still, we may fairly ask what is this thing that Mozart said, in a letter to his father, seemed to him the most important thing in music, and that Beethoven tried, without much success, to convey to posterity by metronome marks.

Tempo is chosen pace; and the crux lies in the choice, which is seldom simple. The composer's indication should weigh with us, but we do not always know what he meant. Palestrina's age gave no indications. Handel often, Bach seldom, indicated it by words; but the words have shifted their meanings; they require as much interpretation as a will. Moreover, these words originally meant to define pace come eventually to describe style; we speak of "the Adagio" of Beethoven's Fifth Symphony though it is actually marked "Andante". Further, the meaning alters with the time-unit; on a crotchet basis Andante is considerably slower than on a quaver basis, though not twice as slow. In this quandary the composer turned to the metronome. Schumann tried, but abandoned it in his later works. Brahms dispensed with it altogether; the only precise indication he gave, in the fourth and fifth Paganini variations, is misleading. If a composer were content with the simple truth as he sees it, he would put at the head of his composition: "This piece takes x minutes in performance." He could hardly get that wrong, and it would settle the whole question.

But that too requires modification, because he cannot see the whole truth. His judgment, based on the mood in which he composed and the eventual contents of the composition, is undoubtedly right; but the actual pace of performance will in practice depend on such things as the acoustics of the room, the time of day or year, the place in the programme, the capacity of the performers, the mentality of the conductor. For instance, Mr. Lener was quite right to take the first movement of the G minor quintet much faster than Mozart, or even Joachim, would have dreamed of taking it, because violin technique has recently made great strides and created new demands; and Sir Hamilton Harty to take the C minor of Brahms very slow in the Albert Hall, where the usual pace would merely have made a muddle.

There are other reasons, too, for a quick pace. Mendelssohn is said to have hurried in order to conceal his players' deficiencies, but we should be better able to estimate the truth of that if we had been present at his concerts. Mr. Coates likes a good round pace, apparently because it adds brilliancy. That is a reason which is parallel to the bandmaster's desire for brilliant brass, even though that involves putting the whole thing up a semitone, with the immense expense and inconvenience it causes. Sir Thomas Beecham moves in an orbit of his own. Tempo is his obedient, humble servant. When he has his foot on "the exhilarator", as they call it in my part of the country, we never think about risks, still less accidents. Of tempo, and especially rubato, its more delicate form, perhaps the truest thing that can be said is that one man may steal a horse and another must not look over the hedge.

THE SCIENCE OF ART

THE fact is, language is an art—not such a fine art as music, because its phrases are not capable of such infinite modifications, but more far-reaching, because we practise it every day, whereas only some people practise the art of music sometimes. Both arts show terrible inconsistencies, though these are more noticeable in language; but they do so because "inconsistency" is simply not in the artist's vocabulary. It is no earthly concern of his what any other artist does, and if it matters what artists have done, it is only because he does not and cannot reason about the heritage upon which he has entered, but has to accept it as his own unescapable personal equation.

Into the art of music, meanwhile, science has never entered but disastrously. The old visual music, as it was called, in which any casual reference in the words to black or white or red, high or low, straight or crooked, was reflected instantly in the tune, was a type, and the frogs and clocks and sheep are the antitypes. Then came "crab-wise" canons, as childish as Herbert's "Easter-wings", and forms, once alive, that outstayed their welcome (like the aria and sonata-form) and produced academic stuff; for music's athletic figure must be encased in clothes cut to order, and not in reach-me-downs.

And now we have modern theories about fanciful scales, and imagined (not heard) harmonics, and non-existent quarter-tones; or, worse, the harmony book that depicts what should be instead of tabulating what is. But music, like all art, is a waking dream; and if there were any laws for dreaming, we should never get a night's rest.

TUNE AND LINE

Now the man who demands, first and last, a tuner is supposed by the faculty to be a poor creature with sadly limited powers of hearing, over whose head the finenesses pass. Perhaps they do, a good many of them, but it is no great matter; there will be time enough later for the fine points. It is supposed that this imperfect hearer wants a tune with a beginning, middle, and end, neatly packed into sixteen bars to go into the pocket of his memory. If that were all, he would make very little of Beethoven's C Minor (about the most popular classic), whose tune consists of four notes, three of them the same, and a great deal of Franck's Quartet in D, slow movement (which he may or may not have heard), where the tune is well over a hundred notes. What he wants is not that it should be compact but that it should be recognizable and individual, whether short or long, whether one voice or many; and when the rest of the piece is true to it, that is line.

Much of Sibelius, some of Vaughan Williams and

de Falla, bits of Kodaly, Szymanowski, Peter Warlock and others give him this feeling of line based on real tune. But with too many compositions of to-day he feels that the man is only calling on him to read a treatise on lepidoptera, not to admire and glory in this particular butterfly. And all the time he does not want a life-history of the metamorphoses and the thousand variations of the butterfly species. He wants to watch the living jewel flit by him.

MUSICAL SINGERS

WITH a very few laudable exceptions, a singer nowadays wishes to display a voice, and this voice is frequently spelt vanity. Music merely demands accurate time and tune. Vanity demands the soprano's high F, an expensive dress, a barrier of flowers and a bath of electric light. Vocal recitals are apt to be legitimatized begging or eleemosynary entertainment or professional advertisement, or some mixture of these. If a prize were given, the award would be as difficult as for the mining captains' ploughing match—"Captain Trevithick's ploughing is the worst us ever seed; but us be giving the prize to he, because Captain Billy Treneer's ploughing ain't ploughing at all."

SUNDRIES

VOCATION

About the age of sixteen a boy begins usually to think, as opposed to larking about with fancies, of what he is going to be. He decides to "profess" something. He thinks that, when he has decided, that will settle the matter, and that he will then "be" a statesman, or a shoe-black, or whatever he decides on. There is no means of proving whether his decision was right or wrong; because, if he turns out a failure, he merely disappears, and we do not know or ask what his profession was; and if a success, we not uncommonly say that he would have made a fine general, or lawyer, or divine, or anything else that he turned his hand to, because what he succeeded on was more character than skill.

The boy lives on and may be happy in his profession, though in some cases he wishes afterwards he had decided differently. In these he says of himself, or perhaps others say it of him, that he "has missed his vocation; he ought to have been a . . ." But how was he to know at sixteen what his vocation was? The fact is, he couldn't know. What a man is fitted for, what he can really do, it takes time for him to find out. Among these boys there is a small number who say to themselves, "I mean to be a musician". Or perhaps they say nothing, but do what Handel did in his garret, or the analogous thing; and we have just read that Jehudi Menuhin demanded a violin at three, and possessed one at four, with a chit from Alfred Einstein when he was twelve, to say that it had not been thrown away. It usually escapes their notice, however, that "Music" is not a profession. You cannot go into it as you can into the Army with a reasonable prospect of dying at least a major-general. It is merely a collection of men and women drawn by inclination and pledged by conscience to make life less drab, for themselves, and, if they can, for others. For the privilege of doing this they are sometimes allowed enough to live upon (without a wife, or a motor-car, or a seaside holiday); sometimes not. They wed their art, they mount Pegasus, they change from the blue room to the brown.

It is probably within the mark to say that there are at this moment 2,500 men and women of England who believed at one time they could sing, and have since found that others sing better, and that there is no living wage for any but for those who sing best. That is the answer to the riddle "When is a profession not a profession?" Not liking this answer, they try sometimes to advertise, a perfectly futile proceeding from their point of view, since, as any man of business would tell them, advertisement of any thing or body that has no intrinsic merits pays no one but the advertisement agent. Others go off on the questionable path of teaching what they never really learned, and they secure thereby that the next generation shall have no better chance than they had.

This is a type merely of the kind of thing that is happening not every day, but more often than it need, to most of those whom musical academies and colleges are erected to start in life, and who were unable to make use of the opportunity. What has happened is that they thought music was their vocation, when it was only their hobby; and they forgot that when a hobby is relied on to win bread, it ceases to be a hobby. They thought in fact that an amateur could be a professional. But the two are distinct.

A cornet-player's son will very likely become a cornet-player; when the father's lip goes the son will carry on the business; that is normal, epic. He will to some extent, however, resent the presence of an amateur either playing for nothing, and so diverting his custom, or playing for something, and taking the bread out of his mouth. That being so, the amateur can do one of two things: he can employ the professional whenever he wants the cornet adequately played, or he can become a professional himself, with all the drudgery it involves. But the profession of even the cornet is not to be learnt in two years' study at a musical college, much less the profession of singing or of composing; they are all of them a life work, depending on "usedness" and character, as well as special skill.

To come back to our boy of sixteen who means to be a musician. He can only be an amateur, if for the reason alone that to be a professional he ought to have begun earlier. But he may be one of the serviceable amateurs, and they are not very common. Inside his actual profession he will find—it is his chief business to find—some way of pursuing his vocation. He is fond of music, but of which form of it? For there are many. He may, for instance, have a businesslike or an artistic or a scientific mind, and be in consequence things as different as a conductor, an executant, or an acoustician. He may have social instincts, and promote concerts with a *cachet* of their own, or those of a recluse and be a librarian or a musicologist. He may be a scholar and write or edit books, or a man of action and run festivals or any of the objects of the Carnegie Trust. He may have an analytical mind and become a great teacher; or he may have a creative mind, and then he will—not, he may—compose, because no power on earth could prevent him.

And the last question, which follows naturally from that remark, is this: Are we to make the path of music easy or throw difficulties in the way? Music was formerly, in a boy, a "girlish" occupation. There was little for him to take part in, and almost none for him to hear. It consisted in his "taking" the piano as an extra, and he usually preferred to "take" sausages. That piano was perhaps locked up in a heavy wooden case, and access to it lay through a party of young critics roasting chestnuts over the classroom fire. The atmosphere has changed; most schools have an orchestra; many instruments are taught besides the piano: the piano stands in a soundproof cubicle; the boy hears anything he likes by wireless; and the young critics themselves, instead of chevying squirrels are photographing birds on their nests. No one wants the old bad days back, but they secured on the whole what the present system does not, that no one should touch music for whom it was not a real vocation.

What we want is another change in the atmosphere. Things will be better when public opinion, both at school and in the grown-up world, says, "Either you take music seriously, or you don't take it at all". This would place a simple issue before our boy who is choosing his walk in life. It would say to him, "You must be, you say, a musician; well, there are two courses open. You can become a professional, which means long and hard work, and if by skill and character you come to the top, the prizes are apt to be great, though the work continues to be hard; if you fail, you may still, with wits and modesty, though with an imperfect education, find out that side of music in which you can make yourself a specialist, and so not waste your life. Or you can enter one of the normal professions, and, inside that, you can, with a good general but imperfect musical education, forward the cause of music in ways which are beyond the scope and reach of the professional."

SINGING AND WHISTLING

NOT far from where I live some builders are at work on a house. For some days they have been digging a deep pit, and in this they now hold a parliament for most of the day. One of them will relieve the monotony of the pleasures of idleness by an occasional and entirely perfunctory ejection of a spadeful of soil, or, when he has to sheathe his sword for lack of argument, will break into melody. Sometimes he sings it, sometimes he whistles it, and there is a curious difference between the two. The singing is, to use the mildest word, atrocious. It is not merely out of time and tune and destitute of tone, but it is a deliberate falsification of a melody he knows perfectly well, because in a few minutes he will be whistling it flawlessly. Both evidently give him equal pleasure, or relief from boredom, and it is clear that, for him, there is nothing more in it than the rest which the vocal chords give the lips, or the lips the vocal chords.

I do not pretend to know what the true explanation may be, but there is one which, if only for my present purpose, I am fain to believe. When he whistles, he is looking at the tune from the outside, considering it as a work of art, as a thing it would be possible to approve or reject; and, in order to come to a decision on this point, he represents it as faithfully as he can. But when he sings, he has to abandon this critical attitude because his feelings are engaged; and even if not very deeply engaged—not, for instance, deeper than "for she had a tongue with a tang"—he is not for wearing them on his sleeve. He is not, in fact, parting with any emotion to-day, thank you, and so he will falsify his tones rather than let you guess the truth—that he cares about them.

Singing is, in its original conception, an act of imparting peculiar sanctity to the topic under discussion. The "nomos" was a sung custom, the "carmen" a sung magic, the "mantra" a sung counsel, the "lay" a sung law. To steal another man's song could once originate a blood-feud. To "make a song about it" was, before newspapers, the only way of disseminating news; and the phrase is still with us to distinguish news of the first importance from news of the second. What the rhapsodists did for the Homeric poems was probably much

what the "kāthikas" do to-day for the Vedas—they
sing the text and then expound it with the speaking voice
in the vernacular, so as to make the clearest distinction
between sacred and profane. The greatest revolution
in music took place when first a melody was performed
for its own sake and not for the sake of the words to
which it was wedded. No one can say when that happened. It is a stage of development, not a moment in history. We see it going on always. Monteverde scraps the
formal entries of the voices in favour of a melodious
ground-bass, thus getting rid of a certain amount of pious
repetition of words. Steffani and Pergolesi stake everything on their continuous melody, and fit the words in
like a jigsaw puzzle. Handel gives the melody broader
structure, and values words as a mere series of well-
or ill-sounding vowels. Bach distributes it between
instruments and voices, and holds that a word has done
its duty when it has supplied him with a melodic idea.
Mozart fixes the spirit and ignores the letter of the words.
Schubert shifts the centre of gravity from the voice to
the instrument, and his successors accentuate this position, until to-day no serious song is written in which the
voice is the first consideration.

During the last century the song and its exponent
have received one buffet after another, the cruellest,
perhaps, from Wagner, when he had his heroine on during
a whole act to sing four notes and to die in silence and
obscurity. Songs are still written, of course, and will be
for many a day yet, but they are no longer borne on the
mid-current of the stream of music. For another kind of
change has come over them. In large halls words are
no longer audible, in whatever language. But it is not

that. The instruments have come into the foreground
and push the voice into a corner. But it is not that.
Composers have forgotten what the voice can and cannot
do, and no longer care to write for it. But it is not even
that. Nor is it the patent fact that the singer devotes,
perhaps, two years to his vocal training where he used
to devote ten. All these are effects of a cause which has
its analogies in other arts; and for a striking analogy
we will take what Lord Hewart of Bury has lately said
of oratory in his presidential address to the English
Association.

After showing how oratory was to the ancients
emphatically a fine art, how the orator was "shaping his
works for all the future and offering himself to be
examined by all-testing Envy and Time", and how the
circumstance that some of the greatest speeches, such as
the second Philippic, were never in fact delivered at all,
rather strengthened the case, as showing that they took
oratory to be the type of good literature; and after noting
that the ancient world could still detect in oratory "a
certain taint of insincerity", he proceeds:—

> But it remained for the modern world to add an entirely
> novel ingredient of insincerity in what has been called the
> habitual presumption that every speech is extemporary. . . .
> But it is one thing to say that a man is required to be
> spontaneous, even though he lies awake all night to be so.
> It is another thing seriously to suppose that, if he success-
> fully takes pains to conceal the pains which he has taken,
> he has really not taken any pains at all. It is obvious, on
> the contrary, that he has taken at least one more pain. . . .
> It seems to follow that, except in private, and by a
> few practitioners, set speaking is no longer regarded

as an art. But neither is it regarded as a conjuring trick. On the contrary, it is precisely the distrust of art and artifice which, together with one other predisposition, seems to offer the chief explanation of the modern temper. That other predisposition is the passion for relevancy. . . . The broadest characteristic of modern oratory (says Jebb), as compared with the ancient, is the predominance of a sustained appeal to the understanding.

Substitute all through, but especially in this second paragraph, "song" and "singing" for "speech" and "oratory", and you have a close description of the change that has come over the singer's art. The set song—we think of the folksong in Holst's "Jupiter"—is no longer regarded as an art. But neither is it—the second "Queen of the Night's" song—regarded as a conjuring trick. It depends on the predominance of a sustained appeal to the understanding, as in a host of things, from Parry's *Lamentation of Job* to Kodaly's *Psalmus*.

The relevant—that is it. We want in the *Messiah* the accent taken off "potter's vessel" and put on to "dash them"; we want it removed altogether in *It was only the song of a bird* (Landon Ronald), because it does not belong: we look for a knowledge of what else Schumann (or Debussy, or whoever it may be) wrote, besides this song that is being sung now; we listen to hear the distinction made, a world-wide one, between *Anakreons Grab* and *Le Martin-pêcheur*; and we do not desire to hear any more *Caro Nome*'s that hold up the action, not even if Grisi were to come to life to sing it. The arts and artifices fail to impress us; we find ourselves taking them as read, and hurrying on to "what it was the man wanted to say". The future lies open to those singers who are, or will be, the first to see this, and to make themselves musicians first and tone-producers afterwards; for most of the difficulty in a song that is called "unsingable" is that the singer has failed to get the hang of the music. (That would be a fine apple of discord to roll down the table at the next meeting of the English Singers' Society.)

To come back to our builder fellow; he sang to relieve his feelings; he whistled to improve his mind. We are most of us whistlers now, and the whistle is mechanical music. But it is an effect of the change to the critical attitude—"every man his own critic" is their phrase—not a *cause* of some new departure in music. It will upset some established industries, as new inventions always do; and they will adjust themselves, as real industry always does. But it will not change the composer, nor the executant; it will be just as difficult as before to get the "development section" in the right proportions, and to maintain that "level of tone" from which all divagations will immediately tell. Nor will it change the audience, or in modern parlance the listener, except to make it a little harder for him, by directing him away from the only solid clue he has to an understanding of the music—in what he can thrum with his "four rebellious fingers and one unthinking thumb".

MUSIC IN A DEMOCRACY

WE are all a little nervous about democracy—a big, genial beast, not impervious to blandishments, seldom fierce, but capricious and multifarious. What has it done with music, and what is it going to do? Music has greater power than ever in a democracy. It is powerful because social: it is the one art that must be social; the others may. This is sometimes taken to mean that music has an effect on morals—let me make the songs, and who will make the laws. That does not seem to follow. Music, like any art, is simply non-moral; in proportion as it becomes moral or immoral it ceases to be pure art. It may be applied art, like the cymbals that clashed for Moloch or Theseus and Hippolyta's wedding march, which idealizes equally marriages made for love or for money; but something else then inspires the emotion, which music only accentuates. It is more powerful in a democracy simply because, whereas one man with a dream can conquer a crown, "three with a song's new measure can trample an empire down"; because all life moves by rhythm, and musical rhythm only emphasizes its pulsations.

Secondly, music must in a democracy be popular. It need not, like cavalry, move at the pace of the slowest horse, but it cannot for long be precious or obscure. *Rima* and *Pierrot Lunaire* say the wrong thing for a democracy: they depend on some piece of reasoning which is not accessible to all. A crowd will listen in amaze to *Seadrift*, feeling that it is a kind of transfiguration and that it is good for them to be there, but not with that enthusiasm with which it follows the changing moods and thronging memories of *A Sea Symphony*. But there is another side to this. Music is not seldom popularized, which means eventually vulgarized. It is administered as papped or spiced food. A little more portamento on a string, a little more blare on a trumpet, a little more crispness in a staccato than the true character of the music demands, and the thing is done, and the shrine profaned. It is a nice question whether that defect, which is to be heard at the "Promenades" and read in books on "Appreciation", is compensated by the good they do.

Thirdly, music has in a democracy not only a broader, but, strange as it may seem, a deeper appeal than in courts or temples. For a democracy lives chiefly in cities, where routine is everything, and everything is routine; and, except for glimpses of the ever-changing sky over his head, the urban dweller's most immediate escape from routine is in music. His pathetic attempt to get it from the street musician proves this. He would rather have bad music than none, because either good or bad relieves routine. Restaurant music relieves the enforced silence of the rest of the day. The gramophone is a godsend because it is always handy; that he turns it on when other people would prefer silence must be considered an accident, though a rather too frequent one. But he would rather have the best music, especially if it will come to him, as in the City churches, or on the wireless. He does not want to know too much about it—that would be almost indecent—just enough to ask for what he wants. In consequence of this he is a prey to fashion, just as those who know no history are a prey to panic.

Lastly, music in a democracy is very multifarious. Different societies and bodies arise for the making of it, the standards and tastes of audiences differ, the methods of the firms that facilitate its production vary, tradition goes for little, and authority for less. The fiat of an archduke, which could retain a Haydn, or expel a Mozart, though it had to bow to a Beethoven, would be of no account to-day. It is replaced by the Press and the law. Meanwhile music has become increasingly mechanized. Not only is it mechanically reproduced, but a certain mechanism has crept into its bones. The virtuoso conductor is a "captain of industry" who goes where he is wanted, and treats men like pawns when he gets there. The members of an orchestra are not so much "understudies" as "spare parts" that can be fitted at a moment's notice. Pianoforte touch is now trained to produce, not music in a room, but effect in a hall. Only the voice cannot be mechanized, so it is crowded out. Of the Press we need not now speak, but in view of a recent debate in Parliament a few words may be said about legislation.

The Bill which was before Parliament the other day, in its actual terms hardly comprehensible, led to a full non-party debate. What is difficult to understand is that the supporters of a Bill which fixes the composer's profits at twopence a copy of his work, and grants to those who pay that sum the right of performance, should say, as the seconder of the motion did, "We are not interfering in any way with the work of authors or composers"; and that its exponents, who propose to run counter to the Berne Convention in requiring that the author should print on each copy the reservation of his copyright, should not realize that that would have a disastrous effect on the sale of English music abroad. Support of the Bill was on two grounds, both of them eminently subjects for a Select Committee, to which the Bill is now to be referred; the first is the protection of the public against excessive and quite unexpected fees for performance, and the other the alleged tyranny of the Performing Right Society. Neither of these can be discussed except on much more evidence than could then be produced. We must confine ourselves here to that highly dramatic "2d."

Everyone knows that, when the organ is played with strings and they thereby are made to sound out of tune, it is not the fact of its Equal Temperament as against their Just Intonation that does it, but the fact that the organ tuning is fixed, and that of strings is not. In the same way, it is not the actual twopence that is going to ruin the composer—he would still be ruined if the fee were many times that—but the fact that by the naming of a fixed sum he is forbidden to bargain. Bootmakers, cheesemongers, writers of penny dreadfuls, street-pavement artists, may all make their bargain, which we may then accept or reject: the composer alone must not. He is to be paid the same whether he has composed a song or a symphony, whether he has toiled all day or come in at the eleventh hour, whether it is his Op. 1 or his Op. 50, whether he knows or does not know his job. This one payment confers the right of performance in perpetuity; but even that does not necessarily secure him his twopence, for the actual performance may (short of a very difficult investigation) take place from a borrowed copy. If he does get his twopence, it has to be divided between him and the publisher (and author of words, if any). His present broadcasting and film rights would disappear; twopence bears no sort of relation to them. All that is left him is his $6\frac{1}{4}$ per cent. on gramophone records, and even there it may happen that he occupies only one side of the record (at $3\frac{1}{8}$ per cent); and all that is left us is to pray that wisdom may be given to the Special Committee.

DOMESTIC INSTRUMENTS

IT is probably best to assume that the fondness— excitable novelists call it the passion—for music has been equally strong among mankind in all ages. Music clutches immediately and tumultuously at the heart, short-circuiting the head; other devices for haling the soul out of a weaver, such as poems and pictures, have to do it tentatively and cumulatively. If it were not so, philosopher and great lady and taxi-driver would not all—as they do—volunteer the information, when you converse with them, that they love music, or "adore" it, a thing they do not spontaneously say about the other arts, though they will if they think you expect them to: with music it just ripples out.

A thing that is taken to the heart like this must obviously be taken to the home. Whereas, of course, no one puts a palette on a handy shelf or a rhyming dictionary in his bookslide, man has always had a domestic instrument. If he did not make it himself, he cared a good

deal how it was made. (After I had written recently
about fipple-flutes, by the by, a lady wrote to ask where
she could *buy* one, whereas the whole point was that
she was to *make* it—or go without.) He cared about it,
then. Old Thomas Mace, in Milton's time, confessed that
his lute cost him as much in strings as his horse in
oats, and advised the reader to put his to bed, to keep it
out of draughts, and to be careful not to lie down on it.
When the clavichord came in, people seized on its
smooth plain lid as artists do now on the fair white wall
of the Piccadilly Tube Station, adorning it likewise
with legends. One of the loveliest of these says—

> Me quo laetar quove plorem
> Indit artifex sonorem
> Me Musarum priscum florem
> Musa morte suscitat.
>
> Rursus ergo vox desueta
> Sonat plorans sonat laeta
> Quandocunque Margarita
> Clavi chordam reserat.

—very roughly—

> Craft lent me tones to laugh or cry,
> Art reared a flower that should not die;
> Now Margaret shall tune again
> My cleffs and chords to joy or pain.

But nowadays we have a large and rather ugly box
on billiard-table legs which we litter with books (so that
the lid won't open) or adorn with a pot of flowers (and
make rings on the veneer) or cover with a carefully fitted

garment (so as not to enjoy the reflections in the fine polish)—such puritans are we!

But it is dull talking about these instruments unless we know how they made their sounds. Take, in imagination, a large fiddle with six strings instead of four, prop it against your thigh, lay down the bow, stop with the left hand and pluck with the right; that is, in essence, a *lute*, and, as on the fiddle, you can raise or lower the note as you feel excited or depressed. Next, bring the fiddle close to your ear, and the fingers sharply down on the strings, ceasing to pluck, and you will hear a faint note for each finger: imagine instead of fingers coming down from above there are metal edges coming up from below, instead of a round belly a flat table, instead of four strings forty, and instead of four fingers on one string one metal edge to each string. That is a *clavichord*: there is no note until you make it by pressing up the edge, and so you can still put a little of yourself into the actual making. Thirdly, imagine that your fiddle has a dozen strings tuned already to the notes you want, so that the left hand, being no longer needed to stop the notes, can now pluck as well as the right; that, with fifty strings instead of a dozen, is a *harp*: you can still put some of yourself into it, because you can pluck hard or gently, and can "damp" this note or that at will, with your own fingers. Now lay the harp on its side so that you can pluck or hit, from above or from below (not both at the same time, as in the harp). The *psaltery* is plucked from above with an armed finger or plectrum. The *dulcimer* is hammered from above with a mallet held in your hand—still a little of yourself in them, you see! The *harpsichord* is plucked from below with a hog's

P

bristle sticking out of a piece of wood; the advantage here is that the sound of the note does not need to be damped, but ceases automatically when the key is released; the disadvantage is that the finger has no longer any means of making one note louder than the next. That power comes back again with the *pianoforte*, whose hammer (from below) is a very complicated thing, and took half a century to invent. With the *piano-player* you resign yourself finally into the hands of your maker (and the young lady aged thirteen who laboriously takes out the splashed notes from the record of the great Mr. X—'s recital); the only discretion left you is that of the organ pupil who pumps (or refuses to pump) the swell-pedal and of the lady who has (or declines to have) peculiar ideas about Chopin's rubato.

Musical historians have not seldom subscribed to a dogma which is a particular case of the argument from design. They praise or pity what they call "the human creature" of a past day in proportion as his "vague aspirations" hit off, or do not hit off, the course that history subsequently took. They picture him as adopting a procedure or talking a particular language in the hope that it may lead to—to what did eventually lead to. It does not seem to occur to them that man does a thing because he wants to, and says a thing because it expresses what he wants expressed, and not because he hopes it may lead to a language in which he will be able to express it. It is so with these instruments. The lutenist did not foresee any of the steps that led to the pianist; to judge from his language, he would have been much surprised if anyone had told him that there was a better berry than his particular strawberry; and when we

listen to Andrès Segovia's guitar we are inclined to think
he had a good deal of right on his side. We shall do best,
then, to think of these instruments not as steps in an
evolution—for since when did any artist concern himself with generalizations?—but as, each of them in turn,
the mouthpiece of an individual and noble art, now lost.
The knowledge and sympathy of Wanda Landowska
help us to guess at the musical feeling of the days of
Queen Elizabeth and of Frederick the Great, and the
insight of Arnold Dolmetsch to reconstruct the outlook
of a time when music was still a beautiful, and not yet a
merely significant, thing. And they do more. They remind
us that music is a thing you make, not that is made for
you. All our mechanized music is only hanging pictures
in a gallery, or stacking poems in a library. The fair
white wall-spaces, reclaimed from the advertisers, and
Harold Monro's Poetry Bookshop, within smell of a
fried-fish shop, are the true opportunities. And those who
make something—fipple-flute or Stradivari—because
they want to understand what they play on, or who
write minuets and canons because they want to clear up
their ideas, have already what listening till the day of
their death will never give them.

THE MUSICAL VOICE

AFTER a long course of dramatic and lyric singers
some of us are inclined in a fit of temper to exclaim
that we would rather hear the housemaid singing on

the stairs. Fits of temper are not commendable states of
mind to be in, and we are ashamed of ourselves, really,
before we have got through the sentence. But temper,
however regrettable, is a part of sincerity, and we do
mean something, though not quite all that. By the
"housemaid" we mean somebody who is well, on a fine
day, with no cares on her mind, with a definite job to
do, doing it, carolling casually and not aware that anybody is taking the trouble to listen. And we contrast
her with the prima donna who has a reputation to earn
or keep, who is subject to colds and tantrums, the victim
of wire-pulling when she does not pull the wires herself,
highly (and perhaps well) trained, and very conscious
that people are both listening and looking.

Three-quarters, at a moderate estimate, of the world's
singers have to be ruled out at once because they have
never been through the necessary gymnastics, or, more
commonly, because they have been through them
without any intelligent thought. They go to teachers
and fancy that the desired capability will be decanted
into them. It does not occur to them that they have to
think hard all the time with their own brains and divine
what the teacher means behind his words, which are,
after all, only metaphors. He can't do the singing for
them; he can only draw verbal pictures for them of what
it would be like if they did do it. I cannot think why he
doesn't use a phonograph more, and show them what it
is like when they do do it. If they heard it in cold blood
when they actually have done it they would take the
last step in true philosophy, to "know thyself". The
phonograph might not show all the fine details, but it
would show the general shape, which is musically more

important, and its great virtue is that by the turn of a
gadget its record can be given back immediately: and
how interesting records would be if taken from time to
time from the same singer and kept for comparison!

That seems a better line for the teacher than all the
talk about diaphragms and nasal cavities. If we could
take our nasal cavity out and examine it both when
it was doing its duty and when it wasn't, it might become
a treasured friend whom we should love to please and
fear to hurt. But as we can't, a photograph of him is
not much comfort; better not to know he exists. Children
learn to say "little" instead of "ickle" without knowing
anything of liquids or dentals. And they learn it, not by
doing something different with the tongue, but by using
the ear more accurately. The matter with most singers
is that they don't hear aright, and don't discriminate
what they do hear. It all comes back eventually to
listening critically, which is another name for thinking
hard. In language we are coming to realize that what
has been grandiloquently called "phonetic decay" ought
to have been bluntly called "aural indolence"; and in
singing it may be that bad voice-production is really a
poor ear. Still, no doubt voices vary in their power of
mimicry as well as ears in accurate reception.

The lyric singer's task lies nearest to music. Though
"ditty" and "strain", to use the old-English terms,
seem to be of equal importance, and at any rate closely
to interact, the strain always has it in the long run.
The ditty at first settled the time of the music, the shape
of the song, and the relative proportions of the accompaniment: the strain has cornered all these claims.
In the songs of to-day the words are merely a concurrent

motto for a piece of music written for its own good reason. We take the greatest pains to declaim them properly, but all idea of singing them has gone by, at any rate in the composers' minds, for they care little about the voice except as an instrument with picturesque qualities and curious limitations. It is for singers now to sing *through* the music instead of *on* it, as they once did. To do this they must be out-and-out musicians, and, feeling the music as it is intended, learning and utilizing its tides and currents, float with it, not battle against it, and show that, however you may delimit its sphere, the voice is still the intensely human thing it always was. It is now more than ever necessary for the lyric singer to be an all-round musician—to know not only the songs of even a large repertory, and many more that he will never sing, but what is going on in the world of chamber music and orchestra and choir, and to get the sound of new things into him as a sort of second nature.

By adding gesture, the dramatic singer lives what the lyric singer does. When action takes the place of words— for there is no real hope of getting words across in any opera—the music suffers a subtle change. Its climaxes being timed to a moment, by the exigencies of such things as scenic changes or the getting a chorus on or off the stage, it proceeds no longer by an inner necessity; transient motifs have to be expanded, salient ideas curtailed. It is, in fact, less music and more something else. And so dramatic singer and dramatic composer have alike to think stage. And since, if our eyes and ears do not deceive us, life is not long enough for a man to be taught both to sing and to act, the singer had better manage to have been born an actor; at any rate, we know what pleasure we have occasionally had from hearing a first-rate actress sing (like the housemaid). (This again, suggests that the opera class at a music college tries too much at a time; would it not be better to act plays intensively, and encourage only those who make some fist of these to become dramatic singers?) In opera, as in song, the music has gradually taken command; the interest more and more centres in the orchestra. The music tends not only to obscure, perhaps to drown, the voice, but to override the drama itself. It refuses to have its climaxes dictated or its flow checked by dramatic necessities; that is what Wagner implied by his "music-drama"—something in which both music and drama should be free to live their own lives side by side.

Since Wagner, the singer has to sing through and even under the music. If the composer intended to drown the voice, he had his good reason, no doubt, but that does not make it necessary for the voice to capitulate, as it would do by forcing. Nothing will ever make bad singing, which forcing is, good. Besides, if the orchestra is telling the story it would be tautological for him to tell it too. Let him save himself, as old hands do, for the moment when he will be listened to. Meanwhile, it is interesting to see how Italy faces this prob-·lem. It holds, and has always held, that on the stage the voice is supreme, but it knows that modern conditions have made that supremacy impossible. So it doubles the voice with some prominent instrument (an octave below, so as not to interfere with it, giving the effect of Mozart's flute-and-bassoon passages); or when one or other of the lovers, at the end, or both of them, are making the supreme sacrifice, they sing in unison (i.e., octaves) in order to show that they have one heart; or, to make it clear that there are two bodies, they drop into an occasional sixth or tenth. All that is against our classical instincts, but as orchestras increase and voices are stationary, we shall have to accept and eventually to like it.

So, then, the musical voice, which is what we have really been talking about all this time, is not some kindly gift of Providence to the body—a capacious diaphragm, or deft tongue and mobile lips, or a velvety larynx—but a mind that thinks music, lyric or dramatic, and thinks hard. A wise Greek, in the days when the poets had said their say and the musicians were entering into their heritage, put it thus: that music is what the instruments make it, no doubt, but the instruments are what the mind makes them. And that applies quite equally to the voice.

THE SPEAKING VOICE

At three o'clock every afternoon a Retriever+Airedale comes and looks up in my face and says: "Put away those old books and papers and come out." About three times a week my business permits me to say, "Leash, Mac", which means, "Go and fetch your badge of office"; and we are off. He chooses, perhaps, Kensington Gardens, where the wind has probably brought down a few dead branches for him to retrieve and lay at my feet, hoping that I will do my part properly;

or Chiswick Mall, where there will be a dash into the
muddy tideway; or, best of all, Wormwood Scrubs,
the finest air in London, except with a north wind,
when it comes laden with gas—where he can chase
imaginary sheep with a swerving, woodcock flight,
and I can get comfortably muddy boots, and pick a wild
flower, which would never be allowed with the tame
ones in the parks.

I usually occupy the time spent in getting there and
back in thinking over how on earth or in heaven I am
to fill a column next Sunday. But, one week, having got
that little matter settled, I eavesdropped on the passers-
by. I wanted to hear not in the least what they said,
but how they said it: to observe, in fact, the speaking
voice. This is much harder to do than you might suppose,
because in the highways, where there is most intercourse,
the din of traffic is greatest, and in the byways there are
few people. The first thing one notices is that the majority
of voices are quite unmusical; monotonous and inex-
pressive. The next thing, that those which are musical
are decidedly so. The third, that most sentences travel
down the scale. The fourth, that emphasized words
are often treated as diphthongs. Lastly, that two notes
some little way apart usually are the pivots of the
intonation, and that the rest of the sentence consists of
passing notes of little tone.

A few instances will be worth a whole paragraph of
explanation. (1) Young woman, narrating some thrilling
experience,

I was just on edge   the whole day.

(2) Nurse to her charge, looking at Mac,

That dog-gy   hurt   you?

(3) Girl of fourteen or so, playing ball with a child—

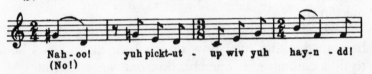

Nah - oo!   yuh pickt-ut - up wiv yuh   hay-n - dd!
(No!)

—which was presumably against the rules.

(Notice the tritones, which Parry picked out as typical of this class of singer.)

(4) Baby-worshipper of twelve, bending over a perambulator—

Look at his   lit - too   frahk.

Written out thus they look as if they were actually sung. But only the salient words—"edge", "hurt", "littoo", etc.—had tone; the rest, chiefly an ill-defined pedestrian gait. Also, it is no accident that all these remarks are of the feminine gender. Women have much more to say than men about a thing that happens, or might happen but doesn't. When the male sex's ball goes "far 'way in ditch", he usually runs and gets it out, without becoming voluble. The man's voice moves in a smaller compass, because events do not excite him so much. He ranges about a fourth.

(5) A stump-orator at Marble Arch ended all his sentences with this argumentative fourth—

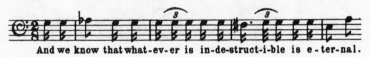

And we know that what-ev-er is in-de-struct-i-ble is e-ter-nal.

(6) An ex-policeman, digging potatoes, to small son making mudpies, after an exculpatory explanation—

Aw! thet's aw rye!

So, too, in church, the compass rarely exceeds a fourth; the voice at the lectern is pitched about G, drops to F, and rises to B flat; in the pulpit the pitch is the same, and the compass a little more in both directions; at the east end the pitch-note is the low B flat and the compass less, a note perhaps on either side.

The compass increases when the voice has to carry over a distance; thus

(7) The porter at "High Street, Kensington", sings out—

"Oi - stick-is - a - turn."

—or (8) in a lively narration; thus two warriors fighting 1918 over again—

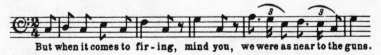

But when it comes to fir-ing, mind you, we were as near to the guns.

A man looking at a caricature of a well-known face
said (9)—

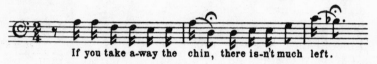

If you take a-way the   chin,   there is-n't much left.

In this last we see the diphthongal accentuation in all
its glory, the thing that Purcell so often records—
in his *How have I Strayed*, and elsewhere. It seems to be
a particularly English thing; a Frenchman usually ends
up clean on his high note, and the German sentence
usually has a trochaic ending. The fact, too, that the
important word has tone and the others are toneless may
account for Purcell's keeping his "divisions" for the
important words, and not putting them, as Handel with
his Italian training was inclined to do, on well-sounding
vowels regardless of the sentence-accent.

Such instances as these may seem hardly worth
recording; but, such as they are, they are genuine.
I don't remember to have seen the subject dealt with
anywhere in English, though there is a book I once had,
and have forgotten the name of, in French. Perhaps
someone who reads this may be inclined to look into
the matter more closely, and tell us what really happens.

THE   CHOCOLATE-MIND

CARDINAL WOLSEY worked, in his day, harder than
any man in the kingdom. When, in 1513, he was not
calculating the tonnage and cost of transports, purchasing

cannon—from "murderers" (swivel guns) up to "cul-
verins" (drawn by 28 mares at tenpence a day each, or
sixteen shillings of our present money)—ordering the
best salt fish from Bridlington and the fattest oxen from
Lincolnshire, securing rebates on hides and on "foists"
of beer, investigating the prices of biscuits, bacon, and
"cauldrons to seethe meat in" or estimating the numbers
required of tankards, platters, or pilot-jackets, he was
writing up *The Boke of the Kynges Armye on the Sea*.
It is also on record that he consumed a great quantity of
sweetmeats. Little wonder he needed something to
steady his nerves and to sweeten all this toil!

What is the toil that chocolates sweeten nowadays?
We see and hear their wrappers, and can make our own
deductions. We see them along most of the roads that
are marked brown on the motor map—a whole paper-
chase of them. And if we follow the trail to the "Pil-
grim's Way" or the "Devil's Punchbowl", we find
where the hares have emptied their bags and are squatting
and munching—perhaps thinking, perhaps not. They
have no thought for others who will come after them;
that is clear. But have they any for the scenery they came
to see? In fact, does one have to "think" about scenery,
or can one merely "eat" it, as it were?

And we hear them rustling in the row behind us at
a concert, and the things they once contained becoming
audible between our neighbours' sentences. One feels
ashamed of minding such a little thing, but one does.
It is not that the sound seriously disturbs us, but that
it takes the edge off our appetite by being so utterly
irrelevant. We wonder what a mouth full of chocolate,
and fingers crackling the paper for more, can be making

of Schubert's Octet, that loveliest bit of Nature. Do we think music, or eat it?

The chocolate-mind has the "lie in the soul". It believes that a chocolate, a "dream" of a frock, and an octet are three very good things; and in that it is undoubtedly right. But it also believes that if it eats one, looks at another, and listens to the third, it will be in the seventh heaven. In that it is equally certainly wrong. For if it really were "in" the octet, it could not attend to the frock; and if it really considered the frock judgmatically, it would not taste the chocolate. So that, since to taste the chocolate is one of the reasons for coming to the concert, it has really secured that its own pleasure shall be less, not greater.

That is easy to see; but there is another and a more difficult point. The heresy is not limited to chocolate-minds, though they are, of course, its chief adherents. The greater part of mankind and, incidentally, of the British Isles, takes what Mr. Dent calls the "Roman" view of music. They consider it to be an adjunct or amenity of life. This heresy crept in, perhaps, from our forefathers who made the grand tour. They ransacked Italy for pictures, originals or replicas, and France for *objets de vertu*, genuine and spurious, placed them in their houses, and never looked at them again. By an easy transition of thought it was supposed that music was a thing you could "place in your house". Unfortunately for that thought, music is so internal a thing, it so gets hold of the soul of a man, that it will accept no second place. People who take it merely as an amenity are for ever outside it. They must toil at it. If you do not believe that, look at the town-bred man being taken round "the garden that I love". He knows nothing of soils and aspects, of rain and sun, of cob-walls and herbaceous borders, of annuals and perennials. He takes it all in the mass, and damns it with some anaemic "Lovely!" And now listen to the neighbour who has driven in from her own garden ten miles away—"I know where you stole that osmunda, but where *did* you get that gentian?" "Oh, do let me have a little bit of this sundew, and I'll give you a cutting of my gazania." And so they go prattling on about things both have toiled at and got a result from, and that are worth anything to them only because of that.

It is working at music that makes it worth while. That is contrary to the usual view, which makes its worth-whileness depend on the beauty, not on the work. There are one or two hallucinations on this subject. It is supposed that people can know too much about music to be able to enjoy it. What such people do not enjoy is to have the things they have known and loved all their lives stuttered and stammered over, or treated unintelligently or perfunctorily. That is one reason why composers, conductors and such big game, are seldom seen at concerts; they would rather be elsewhere, wrestling with the difficulties themselves. It is supposed that a singer enjoys the song when he is on the platform; but he has too much else to think of just then. He is making a speech; and "speeches are things", as Good Queen Bess said to Lyon of Preston, yeoman, John, "speeches are things that we chiefly bless when once we have got them over". But he did enjoy all the varied labour of getting his song ready, and he now enjoys seeing others think it as good as he did. It is supposed

that a tune is beautiful; it is not seen that it is a piece of
wonderfully balanced toil, work that is measured, not
by long hours, but by intensity. Since it comes in a flash
it is commonly said to come from heaven. It does;
but the heaven is in the man's own mind. His weapon
is a congenital gift pointed and tempered by discipline
and courage.

But since there are people who tell us they are "passionately" fond of music "without knowing anything
about it", we have the inevitable question—How are
they to toil at a thing they are too old to learn? It was
the gradual waking up to the urgency of this question
that started sound-multipliers a generation ago. We had
worked hitherto at the language of music with grammar
and dictionary; now we were to use a crib. That may be
tried for a while, but it can never satisfy, because there
is no work in it. A crib is useful to those who know the
language, dangerous to those who don't. Sound-multipliers leave the actual making of music just where it was,
except that they strip it of a little personality and a good
deal of bass.

The desire to understand music is, if not universal,
general and sincere. It is implanted in everyone by the
possession of a voice. The ultimate meaning of symphony
and quartet is that they are glorifications of song; if
instruments don't sing, they do nothing. The best,
perhaps the only, advice to be given (without seeing the
patient) to one who professes himself to be too old to
learn, is Dame Melba's "Don't try to sing, sing!"
And he cannot sing with a chocolate in his mouth.

THE LAST OF THE "PROMENADES"

(1927)

THEIR reading of the law of supply and demand
has caused the lessors of the Queen's Hall to inform
Sir Henry Wood that they will not continue the concerts
of the New Queen's Hall Orchestra after the present
season, which ends with a *Parsifal* concert on Good
Friday; nor will they continue the Promenade Concerts
in the autumn. The avalanche which the weather-wise
foresaw has fallen and it remains to rescue the sufferers.
The sufferers are the whole of musical London; in
particular, the members of an orchestra which will
cease to exist in less than six weeks; and, incidentally,
the singers, players, and composers who had come to
regard the Promenade Concerts as the natural arena in
which to win their spurs.

The "Proms"—for it is hopeless to try to keep up the
pretence of calling them by their full name—had endeared
themselves to us through a third of a century. They
were so firmly established in our affections that we could
afford to grumble, and to say, as we say of *Punch*, that
"it is very poor this week". Things might be poor here
or there, but the thing itself was never poor. It was firmly
based on the sound principle of driving a nail where it
would go; and beneath, there was always a firmly set
purpose, held by both its founders: the furtherance of
the cause of music. General Sir Henry Wood, leading
his forces to battle and handing on to them all the
acknowledgments of their prowess, and Chief of the

Q

Staff Robert Newman, sitting in his well-known seat, from which he could see everyone in the room and calculate the precise effect of his general's dispositions, held the whole thing with a grip that was none the less effective for not being obtruded on anyone's notice. One of the two died, and before his death we had heard our last "Prom." When Good Friday comes, we shall feel like the truant boys and grey-bearded men and women when Daudet's *maître d'école* of 1870 wrote on the blackboard "Vive la France", and bowing his head, waved them away: "C'est fini; allez-vous-en".

When we look back on it, we see that the atmosphere of the "Proms", so congenial to us all, was brought about by a number of little things. Some would say it was the permission to smoke; but smoking has been tried elsewhere without making any difference to speak of. Others put it down to the go-or-come-as-you-please of the actual promenade. Others again to the wise provision of a definite break three-quarters of the way through, which provided a safety-valve for boredom. The fact that these concerts filled a gap between two seasons gave them an impetus, and was of advantage to their general character by eliminating those who are swayed by fashion. Whatever was the cause, there was always an extraordinary geniality in the evenings, which seemed to voice itself in the seductive tones of the boys shouting "Sco-ers", and to emanate from the deprecatory notice about striking matches, and the thoughtful introduction of a fountain to absorb the tobacco-smoke that had done its duty. Most people brought a friend or a family, and everyone made friends with the family of orchestral musicians, who were greeted at the beginning of the season, and often through it, as they came on the platform in their several degrees of eminence, ending up with the conductor.

Theirs was a long and exhausting task. They used to begin in mid-August full of their summer holiday, in high, untamed spirits. They bent to their work and came to their full perfection of ensemble about the time the Three Choirs Festival was over. When the Michaelmas geese ceased to cackle, for reasons beyond their own control, these stalwarts were still holding the breach, but as St. Luke's summer, and their release, drew near, there were signs of physical weariness not to be mistaken. It was a bold stroke to introduce women, about ten years ago, and it was thought they would never stand the strain of rehearsal and concert, and that the tone would go down; they have stood the strain, and the tone is as good as ever. Now they are to be disbanded. No doubt their talent will find employment, but the old spirit will have to be recreated.

Players and singers who appeared at these concerts always found a friendly audience, and that is everything to a beginner. They were glad to be able to appear there, after passing the test of an audition, for it often started them well on their way. And what made the audience friendly was the knowledge, which grew with the years, that they would never be asked to listen to rubbish —either to poor voices or, in the first part of the concert, to poor music. The performers were "edited", in fact; and there is some reason to think that, with the advent of broadcasting, more rigorous editing will have to be undertaken if it is to be worth while for people to leave their fireside to go and listen to music. It is the train of thought which arises in connection with that which enables us to see why the "Proms" have gone.

But Sir Henry Wood has not gone, and while he is there no one need be despondent. He has certainly done more for music in this country than it has been in the power of any other one man to do; and if there is any more fighting to be done he is sure to be in the thick of it. We are slow here to take up new men, and slower still to leave old friends. Everyone will be sorry to see the institution that he made with such care and such a power of work break in his hands, but everyone will be confident that he will build another, and perhaps—who knows?—a better.

PURITANS AND MUSIC

Music is a shy bird; we may walk all day and never put it up; we may top the brow of the next hill and be so moithered with the whirr of wings that we blaze into the brown. I write this purple patch in answer, really, to many letters that have recently asked, "I love music; how can I get to know more about it?" Radio has evidently been at work with the writers of these; there are hundreds—thousands, more likely—wanting to know how this thing that obviously "means" something chimes in with the other meanings of life. The answer is, "What would you do about a motor-car?" (which is one of these obvious "meanings"). Well, you would probably get one, try to drive it (imperfectly), get a friend's advice, read the motoring column of your newspaper, take a few lessons, go and see a motor-track, and do a little thinking on your own between-whiles. You would be a late-learner; you ought to have done all these things when eyes were sharper and muscular reaction quicker. But you may still have the gorgeous feeling, as you shoot across Marlborough Downs (or wherever), that England belongs to you; and you may still get the equally gorgeous feeling that the second Brandenburg comes straight at you, across a couple of centuries, from Cothen, a place you never heard of, where Bach wrote it because *his* Puritans had barred Church music. Music has nothing to do with being a Conservative or a Socialist; why on earth should some people have thought that a dislike of it had to do with being a Puritan?

PUBLICITY

Publicity is good for things, such as a line of steamers or a line in silks; it is bad for persons, and worst for artists, who are conspicuously persons, whose personality, in fact, as expressed in their art, is all they have. They are themselves so conscious of this that they try to express it in other ways. The programme will, perhaps, contain the singer's photograph (in which there is no great harm), but where is the composer's, or the poet's, or the accompanist's, or the benefactor's, if any, who is paying for the concert? It sometimes makes a bald statement—such as "Stradiotsky", or "Hopkinini"—without any indication of sex, or kind of voice or instrument, or of what is to be performed; but there is no music in the name alone. After a hotly contested concerto the violinist will sometimes, either in congratulation or apology, shake hands with the conductor, when all the time the audience is really thinking of Beethoven or Brahms. All these are ways of saying, "You see what kind of person I am", instead of "You hear what this music is".

Publicity cannot really do any more for art than say what is going to be performed, when and where, and by whom. When it goes further than that, it leads to such unlovely sights as Sims Reeves grovelling on his bedroom floor in pyjamas, with a foot-rule to see whether it is true that his name is not, as he fancies, in smaller capitals than those of other singers at the same concert, and in that case to dress and make his appearance. But publicity could do, what it can do, better. It could print in the preliminary notice the chief, at least, of the works to be performed, with information, when necessary, as to how to get to the place. It could send out the full programme as a matter of course with the tickets applied for. It could remember that, short of those people who would willingly pay the few shillings to be allowed to stay away, there are many whose time permits them to hear the one thing they want to hear, but no more; and it would accordingly detail the times on the programme and stick to them. It could state where the music performed is to be obtained. It could take counsel with artists as to its printing and proof-reading and lay-out. Most of these things are done spasmodically, but they might be the general rule; and publicity might well consider the establishment of a weekly pamphlet embodying all available musical information for the whole of London.

People are not exactly unwilling to go to concerts, but they want to have it made easy to do so. They do not want to have to hunt about in this paper or that for their information, and then either not find it, or find it incomplete, or miss something altogether with which, as it happened, the paper was not supplied. But they also do not want to pay so much. They agree with Falstaff about this question of paying. That is much too large and intricate a question to discuss here. But, speaking broadly, common sense would seem to suggest that, the musical community consisting mainly of poor men, it would be more profitable for those who wish to profit to be able to sell 400 seats at a 1s. than 40 at 10s. and give away 360; because the psychology of it would be better.

Lastly, and this is so important that, though only a sentence, it must have a paragraph to itself, publicity might refrain from picking the bud and might wait for the flower.

"THE SYMBOLISM OF MUSIC"

L ET us examine this contention that progress in music comes from the people, not from the princes of Church and State. To begin at home, if the Church had

had nothing to do with music we should, seeing that
we have never had indigenous or even endemic opera,
have had for it no centres at all. It may be confessed
that music did not exactly flourish in the Church, but
it had a continuous existence there which it will be
difficult to show that it had anywhere else. The reason is
not hard to find. The aesthetic mind imagines; when it
is contemplative, as the religious mind typically is, it
imagines in art, when energetic, in games and sport.
If anyone asks why the English are not musical, the best
answer is the still harder question—Why are they
practical? The theoretical and the practical have met here
only twice—in Savoy opera and in the Competition
festivals; and neither of these has advanced European
music. The Church here has been the only mainstay,
and abroad, until quite recently, ducal patronage and
State-supported opera solved what oppresses us to-day—
the question of how the musician was to live. Beethoven,
who flouted the aristocracy (and drew from three of them
all his salary apart from royalties), forms no exception.

Communism is not likely to pay the piper; nor will
it call the tune, or rather, being many-headed, it will
call different tunes. The author hopes that communal
music will give rise to tradition. So it will; it has given
us the Handelian appoggiatura and the Anglican hymn-
tune. But for any fruitful tradition we look, if we read
history, to schools not nations, to individuals not schools.
You cannot, in fact, imagine by committee; imagining
is a one-man, whole-time job, a personal thing even if
he uses it for personal ends.

THE USE OF SATIRE

SOMEBODY was regretting to me, lately, that this age has no satirist. All ages need satire. This age is no worse than others, though pacifist and bellicose, commercial and belletrist keep on shrieking that it is; why, even the harmless Mendelssohn one has just been reading about complained of the "ernsthafte Zeiten" in which he was living. Good health-giving satire is what is wanted, such as this, which might do for The Shepherd in *Pickwick*, or possibly for . . . but we shall see.

> With all his conscience and one eye askew,
> So false, he partly took himself for true;
> Whose pious talk, when most his heart was dry,
> Made wet the crafty crowsfoot round his eye;
> Who, never naming God except for gain,
> So never took that useful name in vain;
> And oft at Bible meetings, o'er the rest
> Arising, did his holy oily best,
> Dropping the too rough H in Hell and Heaven
> To spread the Word by which himself had thriven.

And if the city clerk's wife in *Sea-dreams* did not like this satire "with no pity in it", she did just what a woman ought to do and a man, on the whole, ought not. For he is aware, as she can seldom be, that in times of profoundest peace the world is still maintained in equipoise by armed strength; and satire is one of those arms.

STREET MUSIC

Two goodish cornet players have appeared in our neighbourhood. One of them trolls out recitative-like phrases in free rhythm, and the other answers him at the next corner, eighty yards away, varying his phrase in time, tune, and key. It is the first time in a quarter of a century that I have heard London street music attain artistic status.

DONALD TOVEY'S "ANALYSIS"

What a book it is! It is doubtful if there is any other man in Europe who could use precise words about intangible tones so economically and truthfully, and pass such searching judgments by what he leaves unsaid.

THE MUSIC OF THE SPHERES

That the experience of beauty is an experience of harmony, is a relic of the belief, filtered down from the Chaldaeans through the Greeks to the Middle Ages, in the music of the spheres. It was held that round the earth (later round the sun) the planets swung on invisible cords which produced, according to their different lengths, inaudible sounds. (Saturn, the furthest off, was the "highest" above their heads; consequently, in the Greek musical scale high is "low" and low is "high".)

POETRY AND MUSIC

POETS and novelists have a bad name for their misuse of technical terms. Coleridge's "loud" bassoon—the quietest member of the wood-wind, really—is typical of much. Tennyson's "flute, violin, bassoon" (in *Maud*)—what an ingenious combination! just the thing for Ravel. And the music "clash'd"! (hardly the word). And the dancers were "in tune"—a euphemism perhaps for *not* being in time; and if so, as one thinks of Victorian ballrooms, not untrue to life. Heine has more of the *métier* in him—flutes, violins, and trumpets (more likely, cornets) for the faithless girl to kick her heels to, and drums and shawms (bass-set-horns, shall we say?) for the good angels to groan and sob to. Milton, true son of his father, knew accurately what he wrote of. Shakespeare in his hundreds of references to music was supposed to have made one slip; and now this book shows, prettily enough, that he knew, too, how "jacks" could kiss the tender inward of the hand—so simple, like all great discoveries.